# MAN IN NAM

## Understanding the Cause of PTSD

Chuck Reaves

ISBN: 1497356067
ISBN 13: 9781497356061

# Dedication

*This book is dedicated to every person who wore a uniform in service to their country – friend and foe.*

*Men declare wars; boys are sent to fight them.*

# Contents

# Foreword

As a Naval Aviator, I am well aware of that old axiom "Military flying can be characterized by hours and hours of boredom punctuated by moments of stark terror." Although I've never personally experienced it, but after reading this book, I believe the same could probably be said about military ground combat, and Chuck Reaves tends to bear that out. He has been very successful in capturing the more subtle realities of ground war as perceived by the average grunt; ie the omnipresent—albeit low level—tension of the immediate unknown, personal interactions in shared adversity, and the seeming inability to ever get very clean or—in some cases—dry.

Overlay these more "tactical" issues with the more complex and frequently unfathomable—at least from the average foot soldier's perspective - strategic considerations and it's easy to come away with the head shaking conclusion; "what was that all about?"

Vietnam continues to be misunderstood to this day, and many critics - especially in the media - remain stuck on that 'ol anti-war rhetoric of the wrong war at the wrong time, an illegal and immoral war, a waste of US lives and treasure, and so on. But, just consider...the Vietnam War was an integral part of the "cold war" with the Soviet Union and China, a war which - it should be remembered - we won. And we had the Vietnam War won too before our political leaders snatched defeat from the jaws of our victory.

And the "domino theory" (where one contiguous country after another falls to communism) was just as valid for post-colonial Southeast Asia as it was for post WWII Eastern Europe. Laos and Cambodia were the first two Southeast Asian dominos to fall to the momentum of Chinese and North Vietnamese communism. We didn't get there in time (1963/64) to save them. But we saved the potential "dominos" of Thailand, Malaysia, Singapore, Indonesia, and, very likely, the Philippines, which today are thriving in free societies and prosperous economies. Tens of millions of Southeast Asians continue to benefit from our sacrifices there. Sadly, it could have included our friends in South Vietnam.

Every Vietnam Veteran - like Chuck Reaves and his searchlight crews - should hold his or her head high in the rightful pride of a job well done and a victory won. The Vietnam Veteran in your life, family or friend, deserves your understanding, gratitude and respect. This book can help you both.

Captain Gerry (Jerry) Coffee, USN (Retired)

Former P.O.W, Hanoi, North Vietnam
www.CaptainCoffee.com

# Introduction

"He was never the same after the war."

"When he returned home, he had changed."

"I did not feel the same about him after the war."

"I did not feel the same about myself after the war."

These statements are not clichés; they are indicators of the impact combat can have on people. This book is an attempt to shed some light on what causes these changes and, perhaps, how the families and friends of returning veterans can better understand what has happened - and continues to happen - to them.

He was the boy next door, the kid who played Little League baseball and who delivered your papers. He was one of the shepherds in the Christmas play at the church and was the awkward teenager wearing his first tux to the prom. The war changed him forever.

Post-Traumatic Stress Disorder, PTSD, is a real disease. Prominent people including General George Patton did not understand that and he was relieved of his command for his insensitivity. Since then much study has been conducted in an attempt to understand and address the impact PTSD has on returning combat veterans.

In 2014 several hundred Vietnam veterans filed suit against the Army, Navy and Air Force stating they had been given less than honorable discharges due to their PTSD. A less than honorable discharge is a lifetime disgrace and caused at least one of these men to lose his job with the Veterans Administration. Their contention was that PTSD was an unrecognized disorder at the time of their discharge.

This brings up an interesting point. How can the military protect those with genuine PTSD while not allowing cowards and deserters to escape punishment using PTSD as an alibi?

I am not a psychiatrist, psychologist or therapist, although I am married to one. This is simply one man's story of his journey from boyhood to manhood made possible by a crash course known as the Vietnam War.

"The victim was killed by blunt force trauma to the cranium," is how the movies and television programs express it. In the South we say, "He was hit upside the head." In either case, "trauma" in this context means physical injury. The trauma of PTSD is usually more complex. It may involve physical, mental, emotional or spiritual trauma – or any combination of those.

PTSD is rarely the result of singular event although it can be. Witnessing a grotesque mutilation of a human body that was alive, well and talking only moments before can create enough trauma for a person to experience lifetime of PTSD.

More likely, as you will read in these pages, the trauma (and its contributing forces) creeps up on the individual over a period of time.

Every incident of PTSD has a different genesis so each one is unique. The purpose of this book is to help you understand the process that may have caused the trauma, the "T", of the PTSD of someone you know. By necessity, it has to be one person's experience and in this case it is mine. However, the process was probably similar for the combat warrior in your life.

It is my desire that the pages in this book open your understanding to know how to help that person.

These are the questions that will be answered for you:

- What was it like being in the military?
- What was it like being in Vietnam?
- What was it like being in combat? (NOTE: there will be no gore or disturbing descriptions here.)

Readers of the first edition of this book said things like:

- "I had no idea what was happening over there."
- "Now I understand my brothers better."
- "I was able to explain to my wife what was going on."

There are five reactions listed here that people can choose from in determining how they will respond to returning combat veterans (with examples):

- **Accolades** – such as the planned parades following World War II
- **Appreciation** – when warriors are spontaneously applauded in airports; "Thank you for your service"
- **Acceptance** – "You did what you did, let's get back to life"
- **Avoidance** – choosing not to talk about it
- **Animosity** – openly protesting or attacking

Each of these has a different effect on the returning warrior. Some linger.

Not since the War Between the States has our country been more divided that it was during the Vietnam War. The mere mention of the name Vietnam created animosity and regrettable encounters.

As a testimony to the resilience of the American people, healing has begun. Professional speakers who use their Vietnam experience in their presentations have their peers approach them afterwards and apologize for the treatment the returning veterans received. This book is intended as another dose of balm to further the healing. I have seen former POWs Jerry Coffee and Charlie Plumb deliver their stirring presentations and I've observed the growing number of people who approached them afterwards apologizing for their anti-war activities directed towards Vietnam Veterans. Each of these men has responded humbly and graciously with no hint of animosity.

For Vietnam combat veterans, this book is a voice to tell others of their experience without having to revisit it.

For Vietnam veterans who did not see combat, this is an attempt to let you know why those who saw the worst in mankind – and occasionally in themselves – think and act as they do.

For the Vietnam-era veterans who did not serve in Nam, congratulations. Most of those who did wish they had been as fortunate. Feel no regret or remorse. We did our best to avoid going in-country. Since none of us were in control it was the luck of the draw that determined our roles in the military. We would not take a million dollars for what we learned but you could not pay us a million dollars to go through it again – unless, of course, we were needed. Thank you for your service.

For the draft-dodgers and war protesters, I apologize for my attitude towards you for many years. Neither of us was right; and neither of us was wrong. We were both caught up in an unwise military action that was poorly executed.

For all others, this book is one man's story or, perhaps, one boy's story. While this is my story, it is typical in many ways of what others experienced. Its intent is to help all of us take war more seriously. It may help you better understand the current returning veterans – their thoughts and their actions.

If you have ever wondered what it was like to be in the military, to be in Vietnam or to be in combat, you are about to learn.

Jesus said there would always be wars and rumors of wars. That means there will always be warriors and veterans.

NOTE: Here the term "warrior" is used to include soldiers (Army), Marines, Sailors, Airmen and all others who wear a uniform in service to their country.

# CHAPTER ONE

## Dodging the First Bullet

**M**ilitary radios have a distinct sound. The crisp voices can come across as a crackle. Whenever the push-to-talk key is pressed the sender can be heard. When the press-to-talk key is released there is an unmistakable sound, a "pffft". We would use the key release sound to signal others when we could not risk talking. One pffft was yes, two was no.

I could hear the radio in my headphones. "Station Break four-four this is Construe two-four, over."

The Marine command center knew we had been hit and were not responding. They wanted to know why. I keyed my mike and released it. "Pffft."

"Roger Station Break four-four understand Charlie is close by, over."

"Pffft." "Charlie" was short for "Victor Charlie" or VC – the Viet Cong. In the earlier days of the Vietnam War, the primary enemies of the American military forces were the guerillas known as the Viet Cong. Later they would be joined by units from the North Vietnamese Army, the NVA.

The military phonetic alphabet was designed to improve communication by making each letter distinctive. The VC were the Viet Cong guerillas we fought in South Vietnam. When the NVA came around, we referred to them as "Charles".

"Four-four do you request support, over?"

"Pffft."

"Roger four-four do you need grunts or mortars?"

No reply. I can only respond yes or no. "Ah, roger, four-four, grunts?"

"Pffft, pffft."

"Roger four-four, I will call the 80's and get back to you. Out."

I tossed the headset into the back of the jeep, slid down from the dirt berm and crept over to the Marine tank. The tank commander, Skully, left the top hatch open so we could communicate. He had two radios and each was dedicated to a channel I could not access; I had one radio and could only operate on one frequency. He could not join me so despite the fact that we were twenty feet apart fighting the same battle, we could not communicate.

Between the noise of the twelve cylinder diesel engine on the tank and the jeep engine straining under the load of the searchlight alternator, you would think Charlie could not hear us talk. But he could. He was down the hill in front of the tank so I climbed up the tank's rear fender close to the exhaust and slithered up the back of the turret.

I tapped the top of Skully's helmet three times – our signal – and he lifted off the helmet which contained his microphone and headset and looked up. "Charlie is right there," I whispered loudly as I pointed. "You need to button up. We're dropping some 80's in a minute – watch for my signal."

I crept back to the jeep but instead of taking my usual position on the right side, I went to the driver's side. It would be difficult to operate the light from the left side and it would be even more difficult to operate the radio. I was about to give away my position and I wanted to be able to move back to the better fighting position on the right side of the jeep as soon as possible.

I reached behind the seats and pulled out the headset, put it on and waited. I had taped my map to a stiff piece of cardboard that had once wrapped a case of C-Rations. It was on the ground in front of me and I was using an infrared Metascope to read it. I wrote some coordinates with a grease pencil on the acetate that covered the map and continued to wait.

The radio crackled. "Station Break four-four this is Construe two-four I have 80's do you copy, over?" "Pffft." "Roger four-four we'll take your coordinates."

It was time to talk and possibly give away my position. I keyed the mike and quickly and distinctly read off the coordinates followed by, "One Willie Peter, over."

The idea was that the mortar battery would set their tubes so that the rounds they fired would land on the coordinates I had given them. Just in case they were off, I had requested a white phosphorous, Willie Peter, round be fired so I could see where it landed – hopefully not in my lap. The correct nomenclature for that type of round was the military phonetic Whiskey Papa but on Hill 55 it was Willie Peter.

There was a silence and then a different voice came on the radio. "Station Break four-four this is Construe niner, over." This was the fire control officer for the mortars. "Pffft"

I had given away my position and was expecting a mortar round, not a conversation. "Roger four-four that's real close to your pos, over." Yes, it was close to our position. An unknown number of Viet Cong were creeping up the hill. Now that they had heard my voice and knew exactly where I was, they would focus on my location – I needed to move. "Pffft."

I saw movement maybe twenty yards out. It was too late for the Willie Peter.

I keyed the mike, "Fire for effect, over!"

"Say again four-four."

"Fire for effect NOW dammit!"

Profanity was a newly acquired tool for me. It seemed to be the most effective way to get things done sometimes.

"Roger, out."

I moved back to the right side of the jeep and yelled down to Martin who was manning the machine gun. We had carved a dugout on the downside of the hill below the light. He had some sandbags and dirt-filled ammo boxes to protect him and he was wearing his flack vest.

I yelled, "Incoming!" and he put his steel pot on his head and pulled the butt of the machine gun tight into his shoulder.

I had no idea how long it would take for the mortars to arrive nor did I know exactly where they would land.

Skully had the tank gunner, Scab, move the turret to the right and left as a signal. I assumed he was ready and was wondering what was happening.

We were out of time. I stood, rotated the control knob on the searchlight from infrared to white. The bright white beam that only a Xenon-powered, one-hundred-million candle power light can produce lit up the hill below us and the party began.

About that time Charlie popped some rounds towards the left side of the jeep where I had been when I read the coordinates and Martin opened up with the machine gun and swept the hill. He could now see the muzzle flashes from the AK-47's Charlie was using. On cue, the tank followed Martin's rounds with their 30mm machine gun.

Our mortars came and landed with an unusual precision considering what they had done in the past. It was an impressive sight. There in the bleached white light from the searchlight on the side of the hill, tracers from the machine guns sliced through smoke from the exploding mortars while a cacophony of noises filled the air.

It seemed like Charlie was leaving. I grabbed the mike. "On the gun-target line out one click fire for effect." This should drop another eight mortar rounds on Charlie's escape route.

"Roger."

It took less than a minute for the second barrage to find its way to the hill. Seven rounds fell in the path we thought

Charlie was taking; one fell about twenty yards to the right. Typical.

The party stopped and the only sound was the roar from the two engines.

After a couple of minutes the radio in my headset came to life again. "Sit rep, over."

The Marine command center wanted a situation report.

"Pffft."

Charlie was clever enough to have found a way back and I was not taking any chances - he might be nearby and close enough to hear me. I had dodged yet another bullet.

The immature and irreverent boy the Army had drafted was becoming a man he did not recognize or appreciate.

THE FIRST BULLET

The Vietnam War was building up and the Army was drafting as many qualified men as it could. Any able-bodied male eighteen years old or older was subject to the draft. There were exceptions, of course, for men who were married with two or more children, for certain professionals and for students. It was my misfortune to be out of college when the Draft Board checked in on me and, before I could say Uncle Sam, I was taking a physical on Ponce de Leon Avenue in Atlanta, my hometown.

Males between the ages of eighteen and twenty six make the best recruits. There are several reasons for this. One is that boys and men in this age group are as physically fit as most of them will ever be. More importantly, their brains have developed in every area except one: the ability to understand and appreciate the consequences of their actions.

At this age they are able to understand increasingly complex instructions, learn to accomplish difficult tasks more efficiently and to use tools and calculators accurately. What they lack at this age is the ability to internalize the potential impact their actions might have on themselves and others.

A more mature and wiser man is less likely to run into a firefight and throw a grenade. They have too much "sense".

So the military wants and needs as many warriors in this demographic as possible.

The military's thirst for troops and the stories coming out of Vietnam created an antiwar movement that has not been rivaled since. Rather than go into the military, some boys ran away to Canada – many with the blessings of their families and friends. The gruesome pictures and videos on the nightly news worked to heighten the fear of military service for too many people.

As information flows more freely, the reality of war becomes more apparent. In my opinion, this is a good thing. Combat is not what John Wayne and Sylvester Stallone have shown us. There is nothing to be gained by having innocent people in our culture exposed to the visual, audible and aromatic horrors which create the scarring that plagues some veterans. There is, however, great benefit in having more people understand the real impact of wars - it can only help us avoid them.

There were ways of beating the physical exam, we were told, like putting iodine in a Coca-Cola and drinking it so spots would show up on some organs. Another was not raising our hand during the hearing test whenever high pitched frequencies were used.

The Army was not fooled. As soon as word got out that there was a way to beat the system, the system changed.

The most famous example was Cassius Clay who became the legendary Mohammad Ali. When he went and took his physical, he failed the mental test. The military decided, based on their testing, that he was too dumb to be in the Army. Even a cursory look back at his life and achievements would prove their testing was flawed.

Later he would claim to be a Conscientious Objector and refuse to serve and for that effort, he was jailed and stripped of some of his boxing titles. Subsequent recruits, who declared they were Conscientious Objectors and would not shoot another person under any circumstances, were trained to be medics and were sent into battle unarmed. The white circle with the red cross on their helmet was supposed to protect them, according to the Geneva Convention. Sometimes it did.

By the time I found myself being tested, the rules had changed. If you failed the intelligence test you were automatically in the infantry and on your way to Vietnam. Apparently some guys in the room had not learned this.

One boy was not answering any of the questions on the exams. When asked why, he told the officer in charge that he was left-handed and had been given a right-handed pencil. The officer held the pencil up to the light, turned it around different ways and said, "So we did."

Walking slowly back to the front of the large room to retrieve a "left-handed pencil", he explained that a low score on the intelligence test usually meant a quick trip to the infantry and Vietnam.

The boy taking the test began desperately protesting that he could actually make do with a right-handed pencil and the more he pleaded the slower the officer walked.

With time running out, the officer returned to the boy, held the new pencil up to the light and said, "I think this will do – do you?" The boy grabbed the pencil and began furiously answering questions.

The whole military thing scared me enough into playing the game straight at first and so I was classified 1-A and would soon receive my orders. Soon was sooner than I had imagined. A few weeks later I found myself in a room full of other young boys from every societal category being inducted into the service.

At one point we were all lined up and told to number off by three. The first in line said, "One," the next, "Two," and the third, "Three" and down the line it went. My number was two.

A burly sergeant announced that the Marine Corps needed men and one third of us would go to the Marines. I was deathly afraid of the Corps based on stories I had heard from Marines. The swimming test alone would have been enough for me to consider going AWOL or, maybe, to Canada.

Then the sergeant yelled, "All of you 'ones' come over here". Some of the "ones" had apparently heard the same stories I had and attempted to change their positions. It didn't work; the Army had seen this type of behavior before.

As the "unfortunate" recruits headed down the stairs to a Marine bus waiting outside, I realized I had dodged the first bullet of my military career.

The rest of us were ushered into a dimly lit room that would accommodate maybe fifty people and there were about three times that many of us. We raised our right hands, swore some kind of an oath and were loaded on buses headed for Fort Benning, Georgia and basic training. In a matter of hours the civilian clothes we were wearing would be in a box headed back to our homes and, for the next two years, the Army would decide what time we would get up, what we would wear, when, where and what we would eat and generally make every other decision for us.

On a dark, cold night in February, 1966, thirty-six of us became the Third Platoon of the Seventh Training Company of the Fifth Battalion at Fort Benning. Exiting the bus we were greeted by some Army men with no small amount of yelling, cursing and being told how pathetic we were – the most pathetic group they had ever seen.

These drill instructors, DIs as the trainers were known, wore Smokey the Bear hats and seemed to enjoy the harassment more than they should have. They were anxious for someone to mouth off to them and someone did. What followed was a lesson in obedience that convinced me to keep my opinions to myself.

Sergeant Ash was in his forties, was short by military standards and had a high-pitched voice. He had the accent and vocabulary of a black street kid which made sense since that's who he had been. Over time he would amaze me with his wisdom as well as his ability to outrun and outperform us much younger boys. There were times we would be running, panting for breath and hear Sergeant Ash running ahead of us, backwards, laughing at us and reminding us of the hamburgers and milkshakes that had made us such poor physical specimens.

We were herded into our barracks that night, our home for the next eight weeks, and were introduced to the smell and soot of an old, wooden building heated by a coal-burning furnace. These barracks had been used during World War II and had been maintained to Army specifications. There were enough coats of paint on them to allow them to withstand a hurricane even if the wood had rotted away. The wooden floors were glassy smooth, the result of having been spit shined by thousands of soldiers over several decades.

Sergeant Ash questioned each one of us and when he learned I had ROTC training, I became a squad leader. It was not that I knew anything about leadership – I was nineteen years old, for Pete's sake. It was more about me understanding that there is a right way, a wrong way and the Army way.

Eleven of the remaining men would be assigned to my squad and I would be held responsible for them. If they screwed up and had to do push-ups, I would have to do them as well. So, when a senior person told one of my men, "Drop and give me ten," I also dropped to the ground and did ten push-ups. Obviously I became very attentive to what the men under my "command" were doing and not doing.

PROCESSING

If nothing else, the military is efficient when doing repetitive activities. Our first morning at Fort Benning began with what would become a familiar routine. Some angry-sounding men would roar into the barracks and wake us up. Actually, some were angry. Duty as a Drill Instructor was not considered to be choice duty because they had to be on the job very early in the mornings and stay very late at night. The redeeming factor was that it was in the States and not in Vietnam.

We were herded outside, shown how to stand at attention in ranks and marched to the mess hall for breakfast. Nothing we did was right, of course, and we were constantly berated by the DI's. Fortunately none of my men made any major mistakes and I was spared from doing push-ups that morning.

After a brief opportunity to wolf down some Army chow, we were herded into buses and taken to quartermaster. There we were measured for our uniforms in an assembly line process that would have made Henry Ford proud. From there we were given a simple haircut – every hair was cut to 1/8 inch.

The next stop was another physical to see if anyone had slipped through the cracks that should not be in the military.

For instance, a recruit at Fort Dix, New Jersey who was missing his right hand – the one with the trigger finger - made it to this point. All along the line during his initial physical, induction and swearing in he had been told that his situation would be corrected at the next stop. It turned out that all along the line every unit had a quota to meet and mustering out this guy would have hurt their numbers so they passed him along. From a basic training company, mustering out takes a couple of weeks for the paperwork to process so he became one of the few people born without a hand to become an Army veteran.

After the physical we returned immediately to quartermaster and found that we all had uniforms – amazingly fast. We were issued the exact same things: four sets of fatigues (everyday uniform), one dress uniform, two pairs of boots, one pair of dress shoes, socks, underwear, belt – everything we needed.

Well, not all of us.

Treadwell, a recruit from Kentucky, was assigned to my squad and was the tallest man in the squad. Since squads lined up behind the squad leader according to height, Treadwell stood in line behind me. He was not only the tallest man in my squad, he was one of the tallest men in the Army.

The Army actually had minimum and maximum height restrictions and Treadwell was too tall, he was over the maximum height allowance by a good two inches. However, when he was taking his initial physical back in his hometown, they were apparently having trouble meeting their quota. So, when Treadwell was being measured the medic told him to slouch, which he did, and his height was listed as two inches shorter than he actually was.

As a result, quartermaster did not have any pants long enough for him. Out of the thousands and thousands of pants in the warehouse, none were long enough for the mountain boy. So, a pair of fatigue pants was fashioned for him by cutting the legs off of one pair and sewing them onto another.

Treadwell was promised that three more pair would be made and delivered to the barracks but they never came.

In a mere eight weeks the Army's training machine taught us everything. We learned every marching and flanking maneuver. We learned how to wear a uniform so that everyone looked exactly the same. We learned how to fold everything that did not hang on a hanger, where to put it in our foot locker and where to put the foot locker. We learned how, where and when to hang everything that went on a hanger.

We learned equipment. We were issued a pistol belt and were taught what went where on the belt. We learned how to pitch a tent and how to use a mess kit.

Drill after drill after drill had us functioning as fine-tuned human machines who would do exactly what was expected when it was expected and how it was expected.

We learned the rules as well. We had to memorize our General Orders and be able to recite them at any time. If we missed one, we did pushups. General Orders were supposed to insure we did everything in accordance with military protocol and in compliance with the Geneva Convention.

A well-known General Order was "When captured I will give only my name, rank and serial number."

The most violated General Order was "I will quit my post only when properly relieved". We would be on guard duty during basic training where we would spend two hours carrying an unloaded rifle while guarding an empty building. February at Fort Benning brings sleet and snow in a windy barrage. The guys walking guard would wait for the truck that brought them out to the empty building to leave and then find a dry place to sit instead of walking around in the weather. They would not suffer the consequences of "leaving their post" since no one knew they had done it.

We learned the rank structure of the Army, Navy, Air Force and Marines since rank is everything in the military. There were enlisted men and officers; officers outranked enlisted men. Enlisted men were ranked from E-1 to E-9. A recruit was a Private E-1. There was also a Private E-2 and then a Private First Class, PFC which was an E-3. A corporal was an E-4 and then the sergeant ranks began. A Buck Sergeant was an E-5, Staff Sergeant was an E-6 and so forth. Sergeants were known as NCOs – Non-Commissioned Officers. They had their own culture including the NCO Club, NCO housing, etc. In addition to privileges, each successive rank brought with it more pay and more power.

Officers were, in order, Second Lieutenants, First Lieutenants, Captains, Majors, Lieutenant Colonels ("light colonel"), Colonels ("bird colonel" – their insignia is an eagle) and then the General grades: Brigadier Generals (one star), Major Generals (two stars), Lieutenant Generals (three stars) and Generals (four stars).

Lower ranks obeyed higher ranks. Enlisted men saluted officers and held the salute until the officer returned the salute. Lower grade officers saluted higher grade officers and held the salute until the senior ranking person returned it.

Then the fun stuff began; we were issued rifles. The M14 was a heavy, wooden stock rifle that fired a 7.62MM NATO round and was approved by the Geneva Convention for combat. In other words, it was a conventional weapon. It was the rifle used in the Korean War. The weapons were closely monitored, locked up and counted regularly.

Once we had proven we could tear it down and reassemble it in less than two minutes blindfolded, it was time for training with the weapon.

The first training was bayonet training. Yes, the military still relies heavily on bayonets. We would attach our bayonet to the end of the barrel and practice parrying at tires and other objects. We learned how to "assume a fighting position" with one foot out in front, the rifle held securely in both hands at waist level and eyes locked on the enemy. When we assumed this position we were to yell as loudly as we could, "HEE-YAH"! We were told this would intimidate the enemy. There was a prescribed way to parry, or swing, the bayoneted rifle to inflict the greatest damage on the enemy.

Combined with the hand-to-hand combat training, the bayonet training convinced us we were a formidable foe.

At long last we had what we had been wishing for, a trip to the firing range to shoot these powerful weapons.

First, we had to sit through a day of lectures on gun safety and weapons use in combat. The training would be conducted by lifers, men who had decided to make a career out of the Army. They were all NCOs.

The first lecture began with the now familiar word, "Mens". Mens was the plural of men and many NCOs used it regularly.

A precisely dressed staff sergeant stood in front of us. "Mens, you has been taught hand to hand combat. You knows just enough hand-to-hand combat to go down to the bus station and get your ass whupped."

He continued. "You has been taught how to fight with a bayonet. When you gets to Vietnam, and you ARE going to Vietnam, you will be shooting at Charlie and Charlie will be shooting at you."

The line, "and you ARE going to Vietnam," was used regularly to keep us focused. Only a few of the trainees would actually wind up in Vietnam and none of us knew who they were. For the sergeant, anyone who went to Nam would fill a position that would make it less likely that he would have to go.

He continued, "Charlie will be shooting at you and you will be shooting at him. At some point you will hear a distinct click and realize you are out of ammunition. Just as you has learned you will fix your bayonet on the end of your rifle. You will jump out of your foxhole as you has learned. You will assume a fighting position as you has learned and you will yell, 'HEE YAH,' as you has learned." The sergeant was acting out every aspect of his story indicating that he knew and appreciated the value of the training we had received.

We could all picture ourselves about to go into hand to hand combat with a Viet Cong. With our shirts off and replaced by flack vests, a steel pot on our heads and dirt on our faces, we would face the enemy unafraid. At least that's what goes through the mind of a nineteen-year-old.

"Then Charlie's gonna' shoot your ass because he will not be out of bullets."

He had our attention.

He went on to explain in colorful terms how we would need to learn how to make every bullet count.

The next lecture was on range safety. The rules of the rifle range would be obeyed to the letter and remain unquestioned. This was for our safety. Another NCO handled this particular part of our training.

"Mens," he began because there were multiple men in the class, "when you gets to Vietnam, and you ARE going to Vietnam, you will appreciate what you learn here this week."

He was right about everything – except for the grammar.

We had to "qualify" on the rifle range and our score would determine the first decoration that would go on our dress uniforms. Qualifying "Expert" earned a metal insignia surrounded by a wreath with a hanging bar signifying "M14". The next best was "Sharpshooter" and the lowest passing grade was "Rifleman". Anyone who could not qualify at the Rifleman level would have to go back through basic training again.

Once all of the training had been completed there were three final tests that had to be passed for us to graduate from basic training: the fitness test, the confidence course and standing official guard duty – which Treadwell was excused from due to a uniform issue.

The obstacle course was the closest thing to combat the Army could muster stateside. We were taken out to the course at dusk and given our instructions.

"Mens, when you gets to Vietnams," apparently for this NCO there was more than one Nam, "and you ARE going to Vietnams, you will have to be prepared to fight under all conditions. Tonight you will get a taste of what that can be."

We had spent the day completing the fitness test which had worn us out. Now we had to navigate the confidence course. "You will begin here," and the NCO pointed to a trench, "and make your way to the other end behind that hill without being shot. We will be using live ammo and if you screw up we will notify your next of kin sometime tomorrow."

In fact the live ammo was blanks but we were not supposed to know that.

As he spoke, a water truck behind him was turning the confidence course into a mud bath.

After dark, we crawled the course as a machine gun fired over our heads, flares went off and mines exploded around us. We crawled in the mud on our bellies and then we crawled in the mud on our backs under obstacles. Our pants filled with dirt, mud and stones. The barrels of our rifles had to remain unclogged or we would have to crawl the course again.

When flares went off, we had to freeze until they burned out. When mines exploded we had to find an alternate path. The whole trip took about half an hour and we went in ranks so the entire exercise took about four hours. It was wet, cold and miserable but "basic" was almost over.

We arrived back at the barracks around three in the morning and everyone wore their clothes into the shower just as Treadwell had been doing for eight weeks.

Since he never received the promised additional pairs of pants, Treadwell went through the entire eight weeks of basic training with only one pair of pants which he washed out every night. By the eighth week they were a sad sight. He had done all of his physical training, rifle range practice, the obstacle course and marching in the same pair of pants that were now threadbare and a different color from anyone else's.

That was the week we had to stand official guard duty and were inspected by a second lieutenant fresh out of Officer Candidate School (OCS). We stood at attention while the freshly-commissioned second louie stood close enough for us to feel his breath on our faces. He stared in our eyes menacingly, or at least as menacingly as someone who had only started shaving recently could. Then he slowly looked down our uniform to insure that everything was in order knowing that his job required that he find something not in order.

I'm sure he found something wrong with my uniform but the events that followed overshadowed whatever it was.

After looking me over and locking eyes with me, he made a sharp, mechanical right face maneuver, took one step to be in front of Treadwell, executed a crisp left face maneuver and tried to stare Treadwell in the eyes. He was staring at Treadwell's collar so he snapped his head upwards to lock eyes with the recruit.

His maneuvers were so by-the-book we knew the folks back at OCS would have been proud.

He asked Treadwell a question about "General Orders", Treadwell got the answer right (or we would have been doing push-ups) and the good lieutenant began his slow downward study of Treadwell's uniform. When he got to Treadwell's pants he froze. He could not believe what he was seeing. Here was a soldier going out on guard duty on a prestigious military base in pants that were more appropriate for a homeless person.

Snapping up his head and looking at Private Treadwell's eyes which were staring straight ahead, the lieutenant shouted, "Is that your only pair of pants soldier?" He was not prepared for the answer.

"Yes, sir!" We had been taught to speak loudly and quickly when addressing officers which included officers who had only been officers for a few days.

The lieutenant was speechless. In his Army, no solider had only one pair of pants. After staring at Treadwell for a moment, the lieutenant executed a crisp left face maneuver, took a step in my direction and did a perfect right face turn. He looked at my eyes which were staring straight ahead and hopefully did not detect a slight smile on my face. "Is that his only pair of pants?"

The good lieutenant and I were learning an important lesson: officers are not taught everything in OCS. This would be important information when I found myself in Nam. Being led by young lieutenants fresh out of OCS could be a dangerous thing if the officer was not willing to acknowledge they had not been taught everything.

Treadwell was excused from guard duty.

## AFTER THE BASICS

The final days of basic training find the young soldier thinking and acting differently. After eight weeks of being told when and how to do everything, and learning to do it the Army way, the solider graduating from basic training is a different and usually better person.

The big question during this time is the next assignment. If a soldier leaves boot camp and goes to an infantry unit, they will endure twelve weeks of advanced infantry training, AIT, and, in 1966, be given two week's leave and then shipped to Vietnam. AIT was a tougher version of basic training. No one wanted to go to the infantry but the infantry had the greatest need for replacements.

After chow one evening, I wandered down to the orderly room to ask if orders had come in. No officers were there. The only person on duty was a Specialist Fourth Class, Spec 4, who was there mostly to answer the phone which rarely rang. "Have our orders come in?" I asked.

The specialist looked at me for a minute, smiled, and said, "Officially, no." Then he pointed to a stack of papers on a table and winked. "Can you take the watch while I hit the latrine?"

As soon as he was gone I thumbed through the papers as quickly as I could. It did not take long for me to find my orders since they were already in alphabetical order.

*REAVES, CHARLES JACKSON, JR. US53431422 ASG ENG TRG CO 140 GEN OPR FORT BELVOIR VA*

Alright! I was being assigned to an engineering training company at Fort Belvoir, Virginia to learn how to operate generators. (I was learning to read "military" which would also become vital in Vietnam.)

There are no generators on the front lines; generators are used back in the rear where electricity is needed. Infantrymen do not jump in a foxhole and turn on a light, after all. In the John Wayne war movies he never plugged in anything. This was good news.

I was sitting nonchalantly in the specialist's chair when he returned. I stood to relinquish the seat and he asked the required question,

"Anything to report?"

"All clear, specialist," we smiled at each other and I all but danced back to the barracks.

There was a graduation ceremony for several training battalions the next day after which hundreds of eight-week veterans were given a week's leave. Following leave we would travel to our new duty stations.

My parents drove down to Fort Benning for the ceremony and to give me a ride back to Atlanta. We marched out in a huge formation with the other training companies at Fort Benning with our rifles smartly resting on our shoulders. As a squad leader I was in the front row, wearing my dress uniform and when I looked up at the review stands, I thought I saw my father smile.

I was headed to Fort Belvoir.

## <u>P.T.S.D.</u>

[The trauma that was at the heart of my particular PTSD will be explained in sections like this using layman's terms. This is one person's experience, of course, and is typical in as many ways as it is different compared to the experiences of others.]

*The foundation was being laid for the upcoming trauma. Of course there was no way to know this. In basic training, the warrior is not allowed to communicate with anyone back home for the first weeks. Our civilian clothes and every other reminder that we had enjoyed a life before the military had disappeared. The military intends to become "your mother, your father, your sister, your brother and your girlfriend" according to the drill instructor who greeted us as we climbed off the bus. We were totally dependent on the military for everything. There was a version of the Stockholm Syndrome going on in that we wanted to please our "captors" in order to avoid punishment and, maybe, attain some favors. The benefit was that I was in the best physical condition and had strongest self-reliance of my life*

# CHAPTER TWO

## Fort Belvoir

C lass 2 was a group of two dozen Army soldiers who had been in the military for five months. While that was not much time, it was enough for each of us to have figured out the Army's ways of doing things and how to circumvent them when necessary.

The year was 1966 and it was the goal of most eighteen-year-olds to avoid being drafted into the service. The members of Class 2 had failed in that endeavor and were now working on their Plan B: avoiding having to go to Vietnam.

Each boy had been drafted in his hometown, had passed a physical, had completed eight weeks of basic training as I had at Fort Benning and had been sent to Fort Belvoir, Virginia for advanced training.

Every Army post has a specialty; Fort Belvoir's was engineering. Anyone in the Army who would serve as almost any type of engineer would train at Fort Belvoir.

None of the boys in Class 2 would understand why they were chosen for this assignment since there seemed to be little rhyme or reason for the military's decisions during the hectic buildup of the Vietnam War. And, for the most part, none of us cared; we just knew it wasn't infantry and it wasn't Nam.

When we first arrived at Belvoir we were assigned to a company of more than one hundred boys who would be trained to operate generators. At the end of this three week training, we were told, those with the highest grades would advance to a six week course learning how to perform basic maintenance on generators.

All we heard them say was that it would keep us out of Nam for another six weeks so sixty of us studied hard, stayed out of trouble and made the cut. The others were shipped out.

During our six weeks of second-level training we learned that those with the highest grades would advance to depot-maintenance training which was a four-month training program and would insure we would be assigned to a depot after our training. There were no depots in Vietnam but there were some in Hawaii, Okinawa, Japan, Germany and other attractive places. Not only would this keep us out of Nam for an additional four months while we were in training, it assured we would miss Nam altogether.

So much for Vietnam.

Two dozen of us made the final cut and were sent to a new training unit and were designated "Class 2".

We spent our days either in the classroom or tearing down and rebuilding engines and generators.

Fort Belvoir was close to Washington, D.C. so we spent our weekends at the Smithsonian, the Mall, the Capitol and the other places tourists can go for free. We knew the Smithsonian well enough to be tour guides. Some of the guys, of course, took in the clubs mostly in Georgetown, but soldiers were not welcomed around the anti-war neighborhoods and it was not uncommon for them to return to the post bloodied and with torn clothing.

We were the pride of the company commander. The good captain saw us as the elite students in the training battalion since we had excelled at the first two levels of training and he was sure most of us would reenlist after our two-year commitment ended. After all, more than one-fourth of our military career would be invested in teaching us skills that the Army would appreciate. The problem was we didn't appreciate the Army.

Class 2 had intentionally worked and studied to reach this level. It was our attempt to avoid service in Vietnam. Whenever possible, small groups of us had clustered in the same workgroups to insure we had the best chance of succeeding when we would be rated by groups rather than by individual performance.

For instance, the week we were told to tear down and rebuild a generator powered by a six-cylinder gas engine, the final exam was to start the engine, engage the attached generator and put it under load. If it worked we passed; if not, we failed. We passed. The engine came to life, hummed like a new watch, groaned a little when we put it under load and then recovered just as it was supposed to.

One group, however, started their engine, it backfired and the ten-foot exhaust pipe leading up to the ceiling came crashing down to the floor. They failed.

## An Unfortunate Lesson

There are some myths about the military that are not necessarily true. One is that there are no black soldiers or white soldiers; there are only American soldiers. That was not true then.

It did not take long for prejudices and biases to reveal themselves once we were out of basic training.

Blacks tended to hang around with other blacks, Hispanics with Hispanics and whites with whites.

Having grown up in the South with uncles who were dismissive of most blacks I knew the white prejudice well.

However, I had a father whose viewpoint was completely different and I admired my dad as most boys do.

First of all, my father was a Methodist minister. In World War Two he had earned a Bronze Star, a Purple Heart and a host of campaign ribbons from North Africa and the Pacific.

His father, my grandfather, was murdered by a black man in Alabama for twenty dollars and a gold watch. When the murderer was caught and brought to trial, the family wanted the death penalty. There was some kind of provision in the 1950s that if the family asked for leniency, a judge might commute a death sentence to a life in prison sentence. For my uncles, this was a non-starter. They wanted the murderer to spend a few minutes in the electric chair rather than a lifetime in prison.

My father had several costly long distance conversations with his brothers trying to persuade them to ask for leniency. This was a time when we had little money and long distance calls were very expensive. Some of our grocery money would go to pay for these calls.

Finally my father prevailed. The man was convicted and sentenced to life in prison (and released years later).

While all of this was happening, my father was serving a small church in one of Atlanta's racially transitional neighborhoods.

One Wednesday night the church shook as if an earthquake had hit. A house in the neighborhood had been bombed because the owners had sold to blacks.

It was against this background of God-fearing and black-fearing congregants that he would need to speak to the "elephant in the sanctuary" – the matter of race and his father's murder. Some of the deacons in the church were sure he would soften his stance on race since "his father was killed by that nigger."

One Sunday morning after the hymns, the offering and the special music, my father walked up to the pulpit and began. "You know that my father was killed by a black man. He actually died three times and was resuscitated twice by a black nurse. The killer was apprehended by a black deputy and one of the only black district attorneys in the area helped prosecute him." He paused and then said, "When you want to talk to me about our black brothers, tell me which one of them you're talking about."

He went on to preach a sermon from the book of Matthew and some of Jesus' words.

At Fort Belvoir people were people. If a person was prejudiced, being in the Army did not alter that. If proximity builds contempt, being jammed together with people who come from a different culture can create friction. Arguments would often find advocates for the contenders lining up by race. Fights broke out whenever someone tried to go to the front of the chow line and those fights were usually along color lines.

At one point in my training our squad leader was a black PFC from New Jersey. My thick Southern accent was an affront to him and he made sure I pulled KP and did other nasty duty on a regular basis.

I did not respect him, it's true. It was not the color of his skin, it was his sorry behavior. There was no way he could understand my background any more than I could understand his. He went on sick call at least once a week and was put on light duty most of the time. He never had to exercise with us or participate in any strenuous activities. He did not have to march with us. Even though he was healthy enough to party all weekend – ALL weekend – he was too sick for duty on most Mondays. He observed Christian and Jewish Holidays. In short, he was what we called a goldbrick and was not respected.

The racial divide was always there and was usually just under the surface. Another lesson I would need in Vietnam was an understanding of just how deep the rift went for some people.

## We Graduated

Once we completed our training in generator depot maintenance, we had a graduation ceremony which involved us putting on our dress uniforms, marching around the parade field with others from our battalion looking on and listening to the captain tell us how fortunate we were.

After he spoke, a bird colonel with little to no public speaking skills, made a speech while we stood in formation wishing he wouldn't. My foot went to sleep and I was not allowed to move so I tried making subtle motions to wake it up. When one of the others from Class 2 fainted and fell to the ground, there was enough commotion for me to shake it out.

Finally it was all over and we returned to the barracks to await our orders for some place nice. We waited for a day and then another day and then another.

We filled our days by looking busy when we were around the barracks and trying not to be around the barracks very often. Mostly we went to the PX and walked around or slipped into the Day Room to play pinochle. We saw every movie at the post theater at least once. It was boring but it wasn't Vietnam and it wasn't hard work.

After a week of that, the company commander put us "on duty", a term for finding something for us to do while awaiting orders. Every morning we would fall out, form ourselves into four ranks of six and answer to roll call. Since it was dark in the early morning hours, if someone was missing, someone else would answer for him when his name was called.

Then we would break for chow, be loaded on trucks, taken to a maintenance facility or some other duty station and given our assignments for the day. We would cut grass, stack boxes, pick up litter or do whatever task the folks in charge could imagine.

One day we were assigned to the officer training battalion where the young lieutenants were being taught engineering skills. Our job was to set mines that the officers would have to disarm without them exploding. There was no shrapnel in the training mines so the only thing that would be damaged when the mines exploded was their egos.

We set a bunch of mines and then sat on the side of the field as the officers crawled on their bellies probing the ground in front of them with their bayonets. When they struck a hard object, they carefully uncovered it until they could find the triggering mechanism. Then they would use one of several procedures to disable the device and they would be home free.

It was not uncommon for us to hear a mine explode and some NCO who was the trainer curse out the lieutenant. Normally an

NCO had to salute an officer, even a junior one, and had to take orders from them. The rules were different in the training environment. Some of the NCOs had been in the Army almost as long as these officers had been alive. The opportunity to vent their frustration with a less-experienced officer was just too rich for some of them.

The lieutenant-in-training whose mine exploded would have to suffer the humiliation of failing, the scorn of a lower-ranking man and would have to start all over again.

Once a group had moved through the minefield, we would go back out and set more mines. This went on all day. The last group was only a handful of trainees, the ones who had not yet disabled a mine all day. They had failed, some more than once. If they were spooked by the dummy mines, how would they do in real combat?

While they were going through the minefield for the last time, the staff sergeant in charge of us told us to go out and remove all of the mines that were not being disabled by a trainee.

That was a bad decision. Since we had not been trained in disabling mines, we simply went out, found them and pulled them out of the ground which resulted in a noisy but harmless explosion. The officers-in-training who were in this last group were afraid of mines - which is why they had been too timid to disarm their previous mines.

The exploding mines around them caused them to panic or react in such a way that they detonated the mines they were trying to disarm. They all failed but we enjoyed the experience.

This routine went on for a week, another week and yet another week. We tired of meaningless work.

One Monday morning the platoon sergeant came into the barracks at six AM as usual, turned on the lights, banged on a galvanized steel trash can and woke us up. We had pulled a late night on Sunday night with pizza, card playing and BS-ing. The barracks was a mess and so were we. The regulation was that we had to fall out in formation for roll call with our uniforms in perfect order – "highly polished boots and brass" – and the barracks standing tall: clean, orderly and ready for inspection.

On this particular Monday morning that was going to be a challenge. It would be difficult to tell which looked worse, us or the barracks. As soon as the sergeant left, someone turned off the lights and most of us went back to sleep. Two men made the formation that morning and whenever someone's name was called they yelled, "Here, Sergeant!"

It was obvious from the amount of parking lot that was visible in the moonlight where Class 2 was supposed to be standing that, in fact, we were not all there.

After formation several sergeants swarmed into the barracks, yelling and cursing. They told us we had three minutes to be outside in formation "with highly polished boots and brass" and with the barracks standing tall. This was an impossibility. So, when the whistle blew three minutes later, we went outside in whatever stage of dress we had managed to achieve in the time allotted and fell into a semblance of a formation.

"You ladies think you're smart, don't you?" the sergeant snarled as he walked back and forth in front of the ragged group. "Well, here's how smart you are. We are going to pull your passes for the weekend."

We were not supposed to leave the post without a pass. However, if we took a pass we had to be back at the barracks by midnight which was sometimes difficult to do since none of us had a car and we relied on public transportation. If we did not take a pass, the Army would not know we were gone and we could stay out all night if we wanted. Fort Belvoir was an open post and all we needed to get back in was our military ID and most of the time the MPs at the gate did not even check those.

As a result, no one took a pass. There was, we were told, a file box in the orderly room with our passes inside but none of us ever saw a reason to use it. So, when the sergeant told us he was pulling our pass for the weekend, it meant nothing. So, we said nothing and did not react appropriately which only made him madder. "Okay, girls, we're going to pull your passes for two weeks!" This was supposed to upset us, I think.

A couple of us were shifting our feet since it was cold and we had not taken the time to put on our boots. That, too, was an unwelcomed gesture for the sergeant since we were supposed to be standing at attention.

His voice went up a couple of octaves and he screamed, "We are pulling your passes for a month!!"

At this point Class 2 broke out into applause and we returned to the barracks despite the protestations of the sergeant yelling at us to stay in formation.

Finally our orders came. When we returned from our meaningless make-work assignments for the day we were told that the company commander would announce them after supper. There were animated conversations in the mess hall that evening. Many who knew other soldiers who had served in Germany, Okinawa and other places told of what choice duty it was. I was kind of hoping to stay stateside since I was recently engaged and wanted to spend time with my girlfriend. Still, anything was better than Vietnam.

We stayed close to the barracks after chow waiting for our orders. "Class 2, FALL OUT!" The awaited command came.

This time we were in uniform, with highly polished boots and brass, and lined up in straight lines that would have made the folks at West Point proud.

The captain was not happy. "Men, I have fought this for days. I have called on my contacts at the Pentagon and it has done no good. You are being assigned to a searchlight unit at Fort Sill Oklahoma that is building up to go to Vietnam."

This could not be happening. After all of our careful planning – okay, conniving – we were going to Nam after all?

The captain continued, "I have contacted the unit and they do not have any generators to speak of. I don't know why you are being assigned there." He took a few steps and continued, "We have invested a lot in training you for duty you will never see. It is a great misuse of our training!"

Someone at the Pentagon had decided that since the enemy, the Viet Cong, were fighting mostly at night, the Army needed to resurrect the searchlight units from WWII. The old procedures called for people who had been trained as we had to maintain the large 60kw generators (and larger) that were needed for the old carbon arc lights. There were none of those types of generators in the new searchlight units. The protocol for staffing had not changed with the change in technology.

We were less concerned about the misuse of his training resources than we were about the prospect of winding up in Vietnam. He did not share our point of view.

Stunned, we walked back to the barracks in silence.

After a couple of hours I walked over to a pay phone and called home to talk to my parents. My father, the decorated World War II veteran, would have some advice, I thought. I tried to put the best spin on it. "It's a unit building up for Vietnam," I started, "but who knows how long the buildup will take? If it takes too long they will not send me over because I will not have enough time left to serve over there."

This was wishful thinking. Even if it took months to buildup and I only had a couple of months left in the Army, I would still have to go over.

I saved the phone call to my fiancé for the next day.

We would not be given a week's leave before reporting to Fort Sill. Instead, we would be given one day to pack. We also had to prepare the barracks we were leaving for a formal GI inspection. Almost all of our time would be invested in spit shining the floor, polishing the latrine and putting all of our gear in order. As soon as the inspection was over we would need to pack everything in a duffle bag and prepare to travel.

The Army made another mistake. Not only was the unit at Fort Sill so anxious for us to be there that they would not allow us to go on leave, they wanted us there the next day. The only way to avoid this first move towards Vietnam was to fail the barracks inspection. So, we did nothing and our living quarters looked more like a fraternity house than a military facility.

As it turned out, it didn't matter. The wake-up noise and lights-on began at four AM, chow was at five and we were on buses headed for the airport at five-thirty.

Next stop, Fort Sill, Oklahoma.

## **P.T.S.D.**

*This was the first indication that the military may not care that much about an individual or even an entire unit. Promises had been made and those promises were broken. The ineptitude at the highest levels of the military, the Pentagon, sent a clear signal to us. It did not matter how hard we trained and tried, we would wind up in whatever position the military needed at the moment.*

# CHAPTER THREE

## Fort Sill

My best friend in Nam was Lindsey, another section chief, the leader of Section 45. I was the section chief of Section 44. We met at Fort Sill, Oklahoma where the searchlight battery was formed. He had been inducted into the Army one day before I had so he would rotate out of Nam the day before I left – or at least that was the plan.

Since rank and time in grade (how long the rank has been held) are the primary criteria for being placed in a leadership position, he and I were made section chiefs, the equivalent of a squad leader in the infantry. I had nearly nine months in with my electronics engineering training and Lindsey's military career had followed a similar path in an artillery unit. We were promoted from PFC to Corporal for no apparent reason. At Fort Sill, a Corporal was considered to be an NCO.

Since we were both section chiefs we would go to all of the same training together. We went to map reading school together, artillery classes (searchlights are considered to be artillery pieces) and we compared notes regularly.

We had only been at Sill for a few days when the Old Man, a semi-affectionate moniker for the company's commanding officer, arrived and interviewed the NCOs in his new unit. We were sent to his office two at a time. Lindsey and I were interviewed together and that was when we met. Each of us had achieved the rank of corporal and training companies at Fort Sill considered corporals to be NCOs.

Lindsey had tried everything he knew to avoid military service. He was overweight – they took him anyway; they needed people. He claimed to be an alcoholic - they took him anyway; they needed people. There was no way he could look crisp so he did not even try. Only a few of us knew how really fit he was and the incredible stamina and keen mind he possessed. He hid that side of himself from the brass.

And he had an easy laugh.

We were sitting in the Old Man's office across the desk from the starched, rigid, no-nonsense captain who kept his eyes on the file folder in his hand. He was a graduate of West Point – a "ring knocker". The rigidity of his experience at the academy would be a problem for us in Nam but his training in discipline and military tactics would bring a degree of order that we needed, especially in training.

It's important to make a positive first impression on the company commander because failing to do so can cause him to send the worst possible duty your way. My father had advised me to only answer questions that were asked and to give the shortest possible answers. Apparently Lindsey had not been given this same advice.

The Old Man interviewed him first. "It says here you think you have a drinking problem."

That wasn't a question but a response was expected anyway. "Yes, sir."

"So, how much do you – _did_ you drink?"

"About a pint a day, sir. More when I can get it. Mostly gin."

"Well, we're going to fix that, if it's true. You will be getting enough exercise here to keep you from wanting to drink."

I guess they teach that at West Point. There was not enough of anything in the Army to keep Lindsey from doing what he wanted to do.

The captain studied the folder, wrinkled his brow and said, "You worked for Big Daddy's Sub and Sand?"

This would be the first time I would enjoy Lindsey's hearty laugh as he answered, "Yes, sir; best damn sandwiches in Buffalo. We had 'em lined up around the corner at lunch time trying to get in. Had to sell it, though, when I got drafted into this crummy Army." He laughed again, leaned back in his chair and crossed his legs as well as he could.

Leaning back in his chair would insult the Old Man, we would learn later. He liked strict attention and discipline. We were supposed to sit at attention just as we were supposed to stand at attention whenever he was around.

"Well, you're a section chief now and you need to set an example for the men you lead." The captain probably thought we cared about such things but all we really cared about was getting out of the Army. "I expect you to get your act together."

"Yes, sir," Lindsey replied with a smile that was not appreciated by the Old Man.

Then the attention turned to me. I had a heavy Southern accent at that time and did not realize people from other parts of the country would equate the accent with being slow and ignorant. I don't recall saying much more than "Yes, Sir!" and "No Sir!" as I had been trained.

Afterwards Lindsey and I became inseparable. Maybe that's why the Old Man treated me like he did.

SEARCHLIGHTS

We were a searchlight battery. Since the war was primarily being fought at night, the Pentagon had decided to use searchlights to change the night into day and give the American forces an advantage.

The military, if nothing else, is organized. There is a hierarchy in individuals and a hierarchy in groups of people. A battery was the equivalent of a company in the infantry. A company would typically be four platoons consisting of four squads of eight to ten men each. Four to seven companies or batteries would form a battalion; battalions would form brigades and so forth. The highest-ranking officer in a company or battery would be a captain. He/she would have first and second lieutenants report to them and they would oversee the rank and file, the "enlisted" troops.

The rank and file had their hierarchy. The enlisted would be divided into Non-Commissioned Officers, NCOs, and everyone else. Depending on various circumstances, the NCO rank could begin at the corporal level or, more likely, at the sergeant level.

G Battery of the 29th Field Artillery was a searchlight battery. We had a twenty-three inch searchlight mounted in the back of our jeeps. These searchlights were a high tech version of the ones that had been used in previous wars. They were twenty-three inches diagonally oval and would fit in the back of a jeep. They resembled a table top television of the era. They replaced a sixty-inch carbon arc searchlight that had to be carried on a flatbed semi-truck – and were not as bright.

They were powered by a Xenon gas bulb that looked like something from a science fiction movie. The light had infrared capability so we could turn a knob and an infrared lens would rotate in front of the bulb. Another switch on the light allowed us to change the beam pattern from wide to narrow, or focused. Depending on how far we were from the target, the light could be a few feet or many yards wide and the beam could go for miles. Infrared light cannot be detected by the naked eye. So we could look through infrared binoculars and see what was going on even on the darkest nights.

The experiences of looking through those binoculars would keep me from using binoculars at all for nearly twenty years after I returned home. Having seen the images of carnage and destruction through these field glasses for months in Vietnam, I had no interest is raising a pair to my eyes when I got home.

We also had a single lens metascope, a device that would allow us to use the infrared light to read a map.

The lights would produce a continuous light beam of one hundred million candlepower. For a few seconds, it could generate one hundred and fifty million candlepower and it was powered by a secondary alternator on the jeep's engine. Looking into the light from a close range would cause permanent damage to one's eyesight.

When the Pentagon decided to deploy a new high tech searchlight weapon, they pulled the organizational manuals from previous searchlight units. Rather than rewrite the manuals, they simply pulled the old ones and made their decisions accordingly. Eventually someone would catch on and realize that the searchlight game had changed.

Remember, the military is organized and has rules and procedures for everything. They needed rules and a set of searchlight rules already existed so off they went. Never mind the new technology did not resemble to old technology in any way.

The older searchlights, the sixty-inch carbon-arc monstrosities, were dragged around by semi-trucks and required a 60kw generator for power. Those generators alone were about the size of our jeeps. Our lights were powered by an alternator on the jeep engine. Now we were smaller, more agile and had a brighter light and infrared capability. Searchlight technology had advanced; the procedures had not.

There was no need for sophisticated generator technicians in the new Army searchlight units but we were there anyway and the Army would make do.

### MANEUVERS

Soon it was time for maneuvers – going out in the field and simulating what we would be expected to do in Nam. Often Lindsey's team and my team would be assigned to the same objectives because I was team 44 and he was team 45 and they usually sent us out in two's.

The searchlight jeeps were a new technology, we were the first unit to use them and so we had to work out the bugs.

One night we were out on a hill near the firing/bombing range at Fort Sill running missions when the "All Clear" came and we could go back to the barracks. The temperature was close to freezing and the wind was unrelenting so we were anxious to be some place warm.

Before we could go back the lights had to be locked down in the jeeps and covered according to Army regulations. We had almost completed buttoning up the lights when one of Lindsey's men shook his light to force the locking pin to drop into place. This was the way we had been taught. Somehow, with the jeep pointed uphill on a sharp grade, shaking the light caused the handbrake to release. Since the engine had to be running to power the light, the jeep was out of gear and when the brake released the jeep took on a mind of its own.

The man who had been behind the jeep trying to lock in the pin somehow managed to jump out of the way as the jeep began its trip downhill.

Another of his crew members attempted to jump into the jeep on the driver's side by grabbing the steering wheel and pulling himself in. The windshield frame hit him in the side of the head and knocked him to the ground with a nasty gash for his efforts. However, grabbing the wheel had managed to turn the vehicle's wheels and the jeep flipped over.

Two things were learned from that incident. One was that the jeeps would need to be modified with a locking mechanism to keep the handbrake from releasing. The other was how much paperwork the Army would expect Lindsey to fill out. After all, he had a damaged piece of equipment and a wounded crew member - in that order, according to the regulations.

It did not take long for the maneuvers to become routine and boring. After dark we would be given some coordinates on a map and we would drive our jeeps there using whatever landmarks we could find and our compasses. We would set up the lights and lay them in like an artillery piece by shooting azimuths and back azimuths – compass directions we were taught to calculate using a sophisticated military compass. Then we would wait in the bitter cold.

After about an hour we would begin receiving illumination missions. We would be given an azimuth and an elevation; we would set the lights and wait for the command to turn them on. The command had to be a one-syllable word so the Army had chosen "Flick". "Fire" was the command for cannons and missiles; "flick" for searchlights.

When I heard "Flick" in the headset, I would repeat "Flick" and a crewman would illuminate the light. If everything was right, the beams from each of the two lights would be on top of each other and they would be illuminating our target.

It almost never happened that way. The beams were rarely on top of each other and occasionally were very far apart. We rarely hit the target with the first illumination. This was partly due to the lack of sophistication in the calculations being used by the people sending us the numbers. After all, this was all new to the military.

We would be given the order, "Cut!" to extinguish the lights and wait.

On some hill somewhere there would be a lieutenant acting as a forward observer and he would radio in some adjustments which the fire direction control team would calculate and send us some new azimuths and elevations. We would reset the lights, wait for the "Flick!" command and try again. And again. And Again.

The Old Man made the mistake of telling us that until we could run missions successfully we would continue to go out in the cold night after night.

Lindsey came up with a plan.

The next night he was on one hill and we were on another. We had figured out that the target we were supposed to hit was always a command jeep – a basic jeep. So he and his team went to their hill and my team went to ours, laid in the lights and began scanning the area with the infrared light looking for the target jeep. The reflectors on the jeeps would reflect infrared so all we had to do was use the infrared binoculars to find the target jeep, notify the others and have everyone point their light in that direction. For authenticity we made sure each light was slightly off target.

Whoever found the target jeep would keep one of their lights on the target and turn their second infrared light on the other section's searchlight jeep. When my jeep was lit up I knew Lindsey's crew had spotted the target jeep so I looked for his other beam. We would lock our beams close to that and sit and wait.

After a while the azimuths and elevations would be radioed in, we would check to make sure they were in the general area where we had our beams pointed just in case there was more than one target jeep.

The command post would order us to turn on the lights with a crisp "flick!" I would relay, "Flick", and it was a beautiful sight: four one-hundred-million-candle-power beams close together and the people on the target jeep trying to shield their eyes from the glare of the lights.

Soon we were so good at what we did that we were excused from maneuvers. Our jeeps were assigned to others who somehow could not be as accurate with them as we had been. They were playing by the rules.

We never told anyone our secret and we became known as two of the best crews in the unit. We were the first two units to be excused from nightly maneuvers, much to the Old Man's chagrin. He would get even by making us the first units deployed in Vietnam.

Rumors were spreading that we would be going out in the field for a week on bivouac. No one was looking forward to this, as far as I could tell, except the Old Man. He was West Point gung-ho and he would have a large sleeping tent with an orderly, and a command tent with a staff and both would have heaters.

Lindsey and I would share a pup tent: two pieces of canvas snapped together and supported by two short tent posts. We would sleep on the ground in sleeping bags; the Old Man would have his cot. Our body heat and a candle might raise the temperature a few degrees, maybe above freezing.

Even though we went "heels first", Lindsey's hearty laugh and entrepreneurial expertise were about to become assets for us.

The first night was miserable. We set up camp in the late afternoon, ran missions until the wee hours and returned to our bivouac area, had some hot chocolate or coffee and turned in for the night. We set our boots outside the pup tent and found them frozen to the ground the next morning. There is not enough room in a pup tent for anything but sleeping so dressing and shaving would be done outside in sub-freezing temperatures.

After morning chow, Lindsey and I commandeered a ¾-ton truck and drove back to the rear using the excuse that we needed to go on sick call. As NCOs we had the privilege of doing things like that. Instead of going to the infirmary, we made a bee line for the PX, stocked up on everything Lindsey wanted and drove back out to the bivouac site. We stashed our goods in the tent which left little room for us.

Dinner that night was field rations which was better than C-Rations but not by much. After dinner we would have nothing to do for several hours until we were ordered out on maneuvers. So, we opened *Big Daddy's Sub and Sand – Fort Sill*. We could make deli sandwiches (refrigeration was not an issue), and added chips, fruit and soft drinks. The prices were extraordinarily high but we were the only game in town – or camp.

We found a marker and some cardboard and hung a menu sign from a tree branch. There were a lot of complaints about our prices but eventually we sold out and split the profits.

For two nights we had to stay out in the field without running maneuvers because an artillery unit would be conducting live fire exercises and it would not be safe for us to be out and about. So we were stuck in the field with virtually nothing to do for 48 hours.

Big Daddy's Sub and Sand became a popular place to hang out. We had made another trip to the rear under some pretense and were resupplied with some of the most requested items from our clientele who still complained about the prices.

Master Sergeant Layton was the senior ranking NCO and worked directly with the Old Man. He had more than twenty years in the Army, was typically rotund and ran a fairly tight ship – just enough to keep the Old Man mostly off of his back. I never could get a good read on the guy. He did not seem to care much for the Old Man but as a loyal soldier he kept his opinions to himself.

He and the Old Man would be the leaders of G Battery and would have the company clerk, Corporal Clark, at their beck and call. There was some discussion about the corporal's sexual orientation but we did not much care.

That night corporal Clark came to Big Daddy's Sub and Sand and announced, "Sergeant Layton wants to see both of you now!"

We assumed the days of Big Daddy's Sub and Sand were numbered; MSGT Layton would probably dress us down, give us some kind of punishment and let us go.

Lindsey told me to go ahead and he would close up the "deli". Maybe he wanted me to run interference?

When I arrived at the command tent the only people there were the Master Sergeant and Clark. They were sitting on opposite sides of a small folding table, one that maps would normally have covered. There was a lantern hanging from a rope above the table and the inside of the tent was mostly shadows.

MSGT Layton was smoking a cigar, took one look at me and asked, "Where's Lindsey?"

"On his way, First Sergeant." The Old Man was nowhere to be seen. We learned later he was back at his house at the fort with his wife - where it was warm.

A few minutes later Lindsey showed up carrying his mess kit piled high with sandwiches, chips, apples and fruit juice. With a hearty laugh he served everyone and sat across the table from me with MSGT Layton on his right and Clark on his left.

Layton took a long draw on his cigar, and lifted his hand from under the table. It held a massive deck of cards which I recognized as a double-deck Pinochle deck. "Five dollars a game," Layton said as he dealt the cards. Once all of the cards had been passed out, he took a bite of his sandwich.

Lindsey and I had a reputation for being tough Pinochle players. We played until we could barely stay awake that night and lost only a few dollars. I like to think we did that intentionally.

The next morning the lieutenant came and shut down our enterprise for good. As it turned out, it did not matter. The Old Man finally realized we were training to go to a tropical climate and Fort Sill was anything but. So he called off the bivouac and we convoyed back to the barracks.

Once in Vietnam Lindsey and I found an unused radio frequency and would switch to it every night around five PM, before dark. We would chat and catch up with what was going on and then tune our radios back to the required channel. Whenever we could work it out, we would schedule one of our twice-monthly trips to rear on the same day and play a little Pinochle with whomever we could find.

We had arrived at Fort Sill just as fall was changing into winter. It was cold and windy and there were no trees to help with the wind. Since we were training to go to a tropical climate it did not seem to make much sense to train in such a cold climate. But, Fort Sill is where artillery units train and this was an artillery unit.

Everyone in the unit was trained on how to operate a jeep using a confidence course that was more than scary. First of all, jeeps have a manual transmission and some in our unit had never driven a car, let alone one with a stick shift. The civilian who was training us was a retired military man who enjoyed watching us sweat. At one point he had all of the jeeps going uphill on a long, steep grade. He gave the signal for us to stop. Then he gave the signal for us to move as close to the jeep in front of us as we could. The next signal was for us to shut down the jeeps and dismount – which we did.

The next signal was for us to restart and head out. With the jeeps so close to each other, being on a steep hill and being operated by inexperienced drivers, there were many collisions as we began stretching out the convoy.

Eventually we became confident in what the jeep could and could not do and what we could do with the vehicle.

These were standard jeeps and the ones we would have would be equipped with a four-hundred pound searchlight bolted in the rear above the center of gravity. What a standard jeep could do and what ours would be capable of doing were vastly different which we would have to learn the hard way. The rollover with Lindsey's crew was an example.

Lindsey and I were initially assigned four crewmen each and one searchlight jeep each for training purposes. As only the Army can do, we were trained in everything we would ever need to know about searchlight-mounted jeeps. We learned how to do regular maintenance, make some repairs and, of course, everything about operating a searchlight.

In the classroom we were taught that our role was to deploy to the target area we were assigned and to find the highest possible elevation. Then, we would lay in the light like an artillery piece and take fire direction from our communications center. They would send us an azimuth for direction and an elevation for tilting the light and we should light up the target.

It occurred to us that if we went out in the middle of the night and turned on a one-hundred-million-candlepower searchlight the enemy might know where we were. We would be sitting ducks.

So, one night during a debriefing I dared to raise the question. "Lieutenant, if we go out in the middle of the night and turn on a one-hundred-million candlepower searchlight, won't the enemy know where we are?"

The Army, having an answer for everything, permitted the good lieutenant to answer, "No". The intensity of the light coming from such a small source would make it difficult for the enemy to determine the range and hit it and that turned out to be the case. When we got to Nam and the parties started, the VC attempted to extinguish the light, and their first round would either go over our heads or fall short. They simply could not calculate the trajectory necessary to take out the light.

When we saw or heard the first round, we turned off the light and moved it. If the first round was a mortar round, we would often see subsequent rounds fall where the jeep had been before we moved it.

Fit To Be Shot

Among the other seemingly incongruous activities of preparing to go into a combat zone is the requirement that the soldier be as fit as possible. This includes dental health. So, each of us had to go to the dental facility and be checked out.

It makes sense, of course. A soldier with a severe toothache cannot be the fearsome warrior he could be without that distraction.

The dentist, a second lieutenant fresh out of dental college found some cavities and I was scheduled for a couple of appointments. Since we were shipping out soon, we were given top priority in scheduling so I would return the following day.

In the barracks that night we heard that Sergeant Whittaker, the platoon sergeant for the First Platoon, had a run-in with the Old Man about his teeth. Whittaker's position was that he did not need to go to the dentist; the Old Man's was that he had to be able to prove that every man had gone in for the checkup.

Whittaker came up to our second-floor sleeping quarters and asked who was going to the dentist the next day. There were several of us so we all agreed to walk over together. Whittaker would simply have his teeth checked, we thought, and return to the barracks or hang around the dental facility and read magazines.

When we arrived, we were led into a large room with two rows of dental stations, each row having about twenty sets of chairs and medical chests. Each station had a dentist and the majority of them were like the one I had met the previous day: young and fresh out of dental school. Most of them had been drafted and all of them were officers.

I sat in my assigned chair and the dentist came over looking at my file. He looked at me, looked out the window, looked back at me and sighed.

The he leaned over close to me and whispered, "I have to do good on you or they're going to send me back to the motor pool."

I enjoy a good sense of humor as much as anyone, but I actually paused for a minute to see if he was serious.

A female dental assistant appeared and the dentist announced pompously, "Today we will be filling the cavity on 14." With that, he grabbed a hypodermic needle, pulled my lip and pointed the needle to my bottom right gum. The he looked at the assistant. Without smiling, she shook her head and he moved the needle to the bottom left. She shook her head again and he moved to the upper right whereupon she nodded, again without smiling. He injected the Novocain there.

Apparently this was a game they enjoyed playing with unsuspecting soldiers.

Dentists have always instilled confidence in me by using fancy medical terms and instruments. The chest behind the dentist had the usual twenty or thirty drawers and I expected him to always open the correct drawer for the instrument he wanted.

Not this guy.

While the numbing was creeping into my mouth, he turned, opened a drawer and then closed it. He then opened another and closed it. Then he began opening more drawers faster and mumbling after each attempt to find what he was looking for.

"What do you need?" asked the assistant.

"The silver curvy thing with the, you know, thingamabob on the end."

"It's behind your ear, "she said.

And it was. But he didn't use it; he found a clean one.

While this was going on there was some commotion behind where I was sitting. The row of chairs where I was seated faced the windows and the row behind us faced the wall. On that row there was lively conversation, joking and no small amount of cursing.

Why would I think Whittaker might be involved?

One of the other dentists came over to my dentist and said, "You have to see this."

As they walked away I turned and, sure enough, saw the top of Whittaker's head in the chair where the dentists were congregating.

When the dentist returned to my chair I asked him what was going on. Even though my speech was slurred from the anesthetic, he understood my inquiry. "Some idiot over there filled his own teeth."

It turns out that at some point Whittaker and one of his friends needed to have some back teeth filled and decided to take matters into their own hands. After more than a few beers, they melted some lead and somehow managed to pour a smooth layer of the stuff over their bottom teeth without burning their mouths beyond repair and without poisoning themselves.

A couple of hours later all of us, with the exception of Whittaker, began the thirty minute walk back to the barracks. Whittaker would be required to report to the dentist every morning and stay all day until they had chiseled out his handiwork or until we shipped out – whichever came first.

We didn't see much of Whittaker for a while.

We also had inoculations for every disease known to modern man and a gamma globin shot, a "GG", which helps blood clot faster. In the event we were wounded, this would come in handy. The GG left a lump on our butts; some of the inoculations had other side effects but we were getting all the prep we needed for Nam.

## FAREWELL FORT SILL

Our last days at Sill were busy as we prepared the jeeps for their trip to Nam. They would leave a few weeks before us because their journey would be more circuitous than ours. The windshields and the lights were encased in wooden boxes created just for the purpose. We had some civilians overseeing our work so it was more like having a job than being in the Army.

The jeeps, trailers and trucks left Oklahoma just before Christmas and, with no gear and little else to do, we were given leave to go home, celebrate the Holidays and say goodbye to family and friends for a year.

For the senior NCOs, the lifers, this was a familiar ritual. We had two platoon sergeants, SSG Dawkins and SGT Royal. Royal was a family man who had his brood on base so they would stay close to the barracks. SSG Dawkins would make his way home but was looking for the least expensive way possible.

SSG Whittaker was the platoon sergeant for another platoon, was a seasoned lifer and had family in Atlanta where I was going. He suggested that we could get together over the holidays but I wanted as little of the Army as possible during my leave. Then he offered a free ride back to Atlanta. All I had to do was travel with him as he hitchhiked from Lawton, Oklahoma to Atlanta.

I was not unfamiliar with hitchhiking and knew it would be uncomfortable at best, could take too much time and might even be dangerous so I flew home using military standby. Less than twenty-four hours after I got home, Whittaker called to say he was home as well – it only took a day longer than my flight and was free. He offered to let me hitchhike back with him but I told him I already had a plane ticket.

The other platoon sergeant was SSG Johnson whose family was in Chicago. He booked his flights home like the rest of us using the base's travel office. We would all fly military standby and enjoy ridiculously low fares – all we could afford – and would be near the top of the standby list. If we were bumped for the first flight we would standby for the next one and usually make it home by the third or fourth attempt.

SSG Johnson had always taken the bus home during his twenty year Army career. He would try to fly standby since the travel would be hours not days and the fare was about the same. The men in his platoon explained the standby process to him several times. He was an arrogant man who seemed to resent having younger men trying to teach him anything.

We returned from our "Christmas and Say Goodbye to the Family" leave and learned that SSG Johnson had spent the entire time at Fort Sill. It turned out that when he was bumped from his first flight he could not figure out what he was supposed to do, was too proud to ask for help and returned to the fort. He would spend his last two weeks in the States before shipping out to Nam at the familiar Army base.

We would learn later that he could not read but he would be a platoon sergeant in Vietnam.

Leave for me was bittersweet as it was for most of us. We enjoyed the festivities and family traditions but anytime our minds were idle, Vietnam became the focus.

The morning I returned to Fort Sill, my father drove me to the airport. As a combat veteran he knew what I was heading into. I cannot imagine how I would have handled that if one of my sons had been heading into the hell of war. He was a man of few words so we talked little on the thirty-minute drive. It was mostly small talk, details about when I would be shipping out and what not to write home about.

He had married my mother in the middle of World War II so they were separated for the first years of their marriage by multiple trips like the one I was about to take.

As I stepped to the curb at the Atlanta airport all he said was, "Keep your head down." Then, looking only at the car door handle, got in and drove away.

One of my father's friends was an executive with Eastern Airlines and had arranged for me to be upgraded to first class on the return trip. It was actually uncomfortable for me. I had just left my teens, had just left my fiancé and was on my way to Vietnam. First class travel was over the top for me.

Besides, I was incapable of understanding consequences.

### P.T.S.D.

*A clear message was emerging. Obeying orders and playing by the rules would not necessarily create the best results for the warrior. We would have to determine which orders and rules to follow and which to ignore. In Vietnam this would literally result in life-or-death decisions. The trauma that accompanies this process is subtle and vacillating. Will I get caught and punished for this? If I do it the official way will the results be positive or negative – maybe even fatal? The message we heard was that obeying orders was tantamount to anything else and if it cost us our lives, oh well.*

# CHAPTER FOUR
## Good Morning Vietnam

Something was different. When I awoke the bunk above me was still a few inches from my nose. I was acclimated to the noise and the smell of the troop ship but something was different and I felt a little nauseous.

The bunks, or racks as they were called, were four high in a compartment with seven foot ceilings. This gave each occupant about twenty inches of space between the racks. People who slept on their backs went in face up; those that slept on their bellies, face down. Once in the rack there was no turning over. Several hundred soldiers filled the area which accounted for the smell and some of the noise.

In the fog of waking up it came to me. The ship was no longer rocking; we were docked. The ship's movements which had initially made me seasick had become a natural source of comfort, apparently. A three week cruise was over and the Merchant Marine ship that had become a familiar home was about to become a memory.

Making the transition to calling the ship home had not been an easy one. On the third day after sailing from Oakland, California, we went up on deck and had to look up to see the top of the waves. Since the air below decks was what it was, we were required to be topside regardless of the weather. Troop ships have no reason to avoid the type of storms that cruise ships steer around. So before long I had joined a group of other soldiers who were heaving over the side. We learned quickly which side was best for this activity. Choose the wrong side and everything that comes up blows right back in your face.

After a few days had passed, we were accustomed to everything being gray and metal, to the swaying of the ship and to the monotony. And we were used to being crowded.

On this morning we showered as usual and went to the galley for our last meal of powdered eggs, powdered milk and mystery meat. Returning to our racks, we dutifully finished packing all but one of our earthly belongings into a duffle bag and slung it over our shoulders. Our other possession, an M16 rifle was slung over the other shoulder and we began the climb down the narrow metal stairs to the lowest deck.

G Battery of the 29th Field Artillery would be first group to disembark. When we stepped out of the hatch onto the landing craft we had our first look at a country whose very name had become a source of contention and division in a way that our nation had never encountered before.

Vietnam was a tropical paradise. At least it appeared to be about a hundred yards beyond the docks. Cruise ships routinely go into tropical harbors as they ferry around vacationers on holiday. The docks are usually noisy, busy and grimy but off in the distance the passengers can see the beautiful landscape that attracted them there. The docks at DaNang were crowded with fork trucks driven by robust Americans and all of the manual labor being done by skinny, older Vietnamese men.

The old Vietnamese men manually moved cargo from the ships to waiting trucks. When they thought no one was looking, they would toss a box or crate to one side where it would be gathered by someone who would slip it into a small boat. This was the top of the black market supply chain.

Beyond the docks we could see the lush foliage of the Southeast Asian jungle.

The difference here, of course, was that we were not on vacation and we were not attracted there. Most of us had been drafted – reluctant travelers counting the days until the end of the trip when we could return home.

While we crammed ourselves onto the landing craft, a mean-looking gunboat came alongside. It was a U.S. Navy vessel with a four-man crew and a .50 caliber machine gun mounted on the bow. A dragon's mouth with exposed teeth had been painted on the front which gave it a menacing appearance. The crewmen laughed at us in our clean, unspoiled fatigues with "highly polished boots and brass" – an Army requirement.

I would learn – the hard way - that these were not seasoned combat veterans. Those who have been through real combat find nothing amusing about seeing others headed for the unique hell of guerilla warfare. Those who joke and brag are typically inexperienced and immature.

Once onshore we were loaded onto trucks. I insured my four men were on a truck before joining the other section chiefs on our truck. Rank is everything in the military. In the infantry they are known as squad leaders; in the artillery they are section chiefs. Rank has its privileges. Like the other section chiefs, I had the rank of corporal and was responsible for the lives and well-being of four other men. I was also accountable for two jeeps, two trailers, five M16's, one M79 grenade launcher, an M60 machine gun, two radios and two sets of state-of-the-art infrared binoculars and infrared readers known as metascopes.

I had just turned twenty years old. Only a few months earlier I had been a teenager. Now, after only a year in the military, I had the rank of corporal and more responsibility than I was prepared to handle.

We were driven to a temporary staging area where we would spend the first two nights and begin the advanced education the Army had not taught us back in the States.

Perhaps the Army did not know the real deal or maybe this is just the way things are sometimes. Perhaps the real world of combat cannot be taught in a classroom or training camp. Guerrilla warfare was relatively new to us as it has been for armies in the past. By definition, guerrilla warfare is unconventional warfare. When something is unconventional it is new.

In fact, during the American Revolution the ragtag Patriots used Guerilla warfare to defeat one of the most powerful armies in the world. The rules of conventional warfare at that time required soldiers to stand in straight rows and fire at their enemy. The rules also stated that killing officers was off limits. Officers would stand in the midst of a battle and direct their armies assured that no one on the other side would deliberately target them.

Americans fired from behind trees wherever the tree happened to be and targeted officers. They understood that taking out the leadership was more important than taking out the followers.

The rules of conventional warfare would prove costly to the American presence in Vietnam. The Viet Cong, the VC, Charlie, the Gooks would not play by the rules primarily because few of them even knew the rules existed.

We were trained in conventional warfare which included the limited guerrilla tactics of the previous war, the Korean War. We had rules of engagement under the Geneva Convention, rules we would have to obey or suffer the consequences. Before long, we would be violating the rules of the Geneva Convention on a regular basis because the consequences for obeying them in a guerilla war were worse that the punishment for disobeying.

## DaNang

DaNang was a U.S. Marine stronghold. We were Army. There is no love lost between Marines (Jarheads) and the Army (Doggies). We were at their mercy for almost everything. This would prove to be a challenge the entire time we were in Nam.

The staging area we were assigned was a couple of old tents and a ditch. The ditch was where we were to go if we were attacked. It was designed for forty men; there were eighty of us. We slept shoulder to shoulder. It turned out that continuously bumping into each other on the troop ship had been valuable conditioning for this environment.

When the signal was given for us to practice running to the ditch, we quickly realized we would not all fit in it but we tried anyway and wedged ourselves in just as we would do if we were actually being attacked. And, if we were attacked, we would fire our rifles from this position except for one thing, we had no bullets.

The most significant issue for us was ammunition. We were one of the first units in country to be armed with the M16 – "the most effective jungle fighting weapon ever made". The VC referred to it as "Black Death". In fact, we had been issued these fine weapons only days before we shipped out. We barely knew the weapons we were carrying and we had no bullets for them.

We had no experience with the M16s on the rifle range except that in order to meet some Army regulation, just before shipping out, we were taken to the rifle range, given one clip and told to sight in our weapons. Since everyone's head is shaped differently, the sights on a rifle need to be adjusted so that what the shooter sees in their sights is what the bullet will hit. It usually takes more than one clip but that's all we had.

Another problem with the firing range experience was that we did not have the smaller cleaning pads the M16 required, only the larger ones for the M14s we had been using which were too large for the M16 and we could not swab out the oil used in cleaning the weapon. So, every time we fired the rifle a spurt of oil came back in our eyes. Most people closed their eyes during the exercise. Since I wear glasses, I kept my eyes open but could not see much through the oil that soon covered the lens.

How does anyone adjust the sights on their rifle with their eyes closed?

I don't think any of us hit our targets but we were classified as qualified anyway. After all, if we did not qualify we could not be shipped out to a combat zone. That was one of the rules. It became apparent that rules were made to be broken and if the military could break them, perhaps we could as well.

These were the weapons we would carry from America to Vietnam to accomplish our mission and to defend ourselves. Except that we had no bullets.

Instead of wood, the M16 was made of a virtually unbreakable black composite. It was less likely to rust or rot. It was lighter weight, shorter and fired a smaller round than its older brother, the

M14 that everyone else in Vietnam was using. In fact, the Marines would still be using the M14 when I left Vietnam a year later.

As a result, there was no M16 ammunition in DaNang. We were in a combat zone with an advanced weapon and no ammunition.

For practice, the alarm was given that we were under attack and we practiced running to the ditch with our unloaded M16s.

So, here we were, stuck in a ditch, shoulder to shoulder and exposed from the waist up. If the enemy had been around we would have looked like one of the arcade games at the carnival and would have been easy to take out. We would have had no more capability to fire back than the arcade figures.

Someone began yelling, "Bang, bang, bang," and soon the rest of us joined in. The sergeant in charge – a "lifer" - came unglued. He began cursing us, telling us this was not funny and hitting any-one who could not dodge his hand. The fact that there were no enemies around, no incoming fire and the fact that some Marines only a few yards away were eating and laughing at us did not seem to bother the good sergeant.

At one point, someone yelled, "I'm hit! I'm hit!" Since there were no incoming rounds, we found this to be creatively amusing. As he fell backwards to the ground clutching his chest, a couple of other guys opened their first aid kits and began bandaging the "wounded" soldier. The sergeant went ballistic as the Marines fell over laughing.

We were inexperienced and immature.

That would change.

BASE CAMP

Finally we were assigned a base camp area near the airbase in DaNang. It was a place the Marines did not want. By the way, when the Marines do not want something, it is usually not worth having.

A base camp has five important structures: barracks (hooches) for sleeping, an orderly room for the command center, a supply tent, a mess hall and a latrine. This base camp had the remains of what had once been a hooch. That was it.

Hooch was a term for housing. There were two types of hooches in Vietnam: ours and the locals. Ours were built off the ground using 4X8 sheets of plywood. Every man had a four-by-eight foot section to call his own. There would be a plywood floor, a four-foot high plywood wall and a tin roof. If screening was available, it would fill the space from the top of the plywood wall to the roof.

Sergeant Whittaker was a career Army man. He had attained higher ranks during his career but always managed to get in trouble and get busted back to Private where he would restart his climb up the ladder. He was no stranger to the ways of the military and the devious ways of working around them. I would learn some valuable - if inappropriate - tactics from him.

When we first boarded the troop ship back in California, he made a beeline to the room where poker games were played. There were three tables with eight or ten soldiers playing blackjack at each table. Whittaker took a seat at one of the tables. Three days later we set sail and I realized Whittaker was sitting next to the wall and not playing poker.

"So, lost all your money?" I asked.

"I own the tables," he replied.

That was Whittaker. Three days onboard a troop ship and he was a casino owner.

Most of us, including the officers, stood around the sorry base camp not knowing what to do. Whittaker knew. He took a couple of cases of jungle fatigues, threw them in a truck and he and a driver drove away. Jungle fatigues were new and everyone wanted them. They are used now in Iraq and Afghanistan; back then they were rare.

The driver of the truck returned a couple of hours later without Whittaker or the jungle fatigues.

About sundown Whittaker returned with a low-boy semi-truck loaded with lumber, plumbing and electrical equipment – everything needed to build a base camp. He had traded some of our coveted jungle fatigues, the only ones in all of DaNang, for the materials – and the truck. The Old Man, our battery commander made him give back the truck. It had a serial number.

In less than a week we had a complete base camp except that we shared a mess hall with a Marine unit.

So, a week later, base camp at least appeared to be in order: an open space between two rows of structures: hooches for sleeping, command post hooch and tents for supplies and for maintaining the vehicles. And, of course, a shower and a latrine. The jeeps and trucks had found their way to us and once we had unpacked and serviced them we were ready.

THE DUMP

A couple of times a week a truck would take a load of trash to the dump. Whittaker suggested that I volunteer to ride shot-gun on one of the garbage runs. This was a task for a low-ranking individual. But, if Whittaker suggested something, I usually found it advantageous to do it.

The dump was about thirty minutes from base camp. Two of us stood guard standing in the back of the truck with the trash. Most of the travel was through the populated area of DaNang and was not considered to be dangerous. Once outside the city limits we had to be on the lookout for snipers though there were few reports of problems.

What Whittaker wanted me to learn was at the dump.

Approaching the expanse of bare, flat land, we saw how people lived who survived off of the Americans' waste. Their living quarters were made from discarded plastic tarps, cardboard and, for the more affluent, tin.

The stench of human waste and rotting garbage did not seem to bother them at all. Water was retrieved from a near-stagnant pond a half mile away. It was transported by the women while the men sat and watched. A momma-san would have a long board balanced on her shoulder with buckets of water hanging from each end. She would create a rhythm with the board so that it would bounce and, while in the air, the old lady could take a step. The board would return to her shoulder, bounce and she would take another step. She would walk with this rhythmic pattern about as fast as I could walk.

The men sat and watched even though they had nothing else to do. My disgust for the way the men treated the women would grow. It would make it easier to pull the trigger in the future.

As we slowed to approach the dump, people came from every direction trying to outrun the others in order to be the first on the truck. They wanted the prime stuff.

Before the truck came to a full stop the trash was covered with people in black pajamas and pointed straw hats jabbering in Vietnamese. In less time than I thought it could happen, only scraps and dirt remained on the truck.

That's when it happened.

An old woman of some undeterminable age clumsily climbed up on the truck with a piece of cardboard. She diligently swept the bed of the truck as if it were the presidential palace. As she swept I saw what appeared to be her granddaughter standing behind the truck. When we locked eyes, she smiled the faintest of smiles. She was maybe ten years old and she had already experienced more than most people would in a lifetime.

She was clean. She was unlike the others. Her clean hair, face, hands and clothes were juxtaposed against the background of the dump behind her. Her clothes were American, obviously something from a previous trash run. But her clothes were as clean as her face. I wondered where her mother and father were. Was her father one of the men who would attack Americans? Was her mother dead or alive? Why would any parent leave such a precious child to live in this squalor with an old feeble woman?

I took her picture with my Instamatic camera. The image haunts me now.

Once the truck bed was clean, the old woman stood up as much as she could and stared at us. "She expects money," the driver said. I reached in my pocket. I knew I could not give American script to the locals and I had changed some money into Vietnamese currency. I gave her the equivalent of about twenty-five cents and quickly learned I had overpaid. She normally received less. I was rewarded with a broad toothless smile.

After laboriously climbing off the truck, she took the hand of the little girl and hurried away. The girl looked back over her shoulder at me – more with curiosity than anything else.

Maybe Whittaker knew or maybe not. I would need to experience this tender side of the culture to help me cling to sanity in the months to come.

In the open country on the road back to base camp, at one point the driver blew the horn as we passed a plaster house up on a slight rise. The young girl on the porch lifted her shirt to expose her breasts, smiled and waved for us to come up for a visit. The truck never slowed.

There were reports that places like this were the last places GI's ever saw.

The Old Man

Captain Hayworth, the ring knocker, our battery commander, had not suffered the indignity of the troop ship but, instead, had flown over to Nam. He was arrogant, opinionated and did everything strictly by the book. He and I would have some fierce conversations in the coming months including his efforts to have me court martialed. He was impossible to respect and even more difficult to like. It was apparent he had ticked off someone in his past to have been assigned the command of G Battery of the 29th Field Artillery in DaNang, South Vietnam.

His disdain for Whittaker was obvious. Even more apparent was his jealousy of the reception Whittaker and his truck had received.

To this day I do not know what I did to get on the wrong side of the Old Man. If there was a way he could make Nam worse for me, he did it. Ultimately and inadvertently, I would have the last say.

By now we had some bullets but were not allowed to wear the more comfortable jungle fatigues. They were lighter weight, had larger pockets and the shirts were worn outside the belt, not tucked in. Because they did not have name tags sewn on them, we could not wear them. So, in the tropical heat of Vietnam, we were wearing the same fatigues our counterparts were wearing in Germany. It was February. When you see pictures from the Vietnam War, you see men in tee shirts and shirtless. There is a reason for that. The fatigues were unbearably hot.

When the first orders for G Battery were received, the Old Man made sure that I and my four guys were the first deployed.

We were sent a short distance away to Hill 327.

Hill 327

Military maps are topographical. They show permanent land-marks, like roads and rivers and the elevation of hills. The highest point of each hill on the map is shown in meters. Hill 327 was 327 meters high. In fact, it was one of the highest hills around DaNang.

Strategically, it made sense for us to find a higher elevation so the light could cover a larger area. We arrived on the hill and I checked in with the highest ranking Marine officer, a second lieutenant. I swear he must have been separated at birth from the Old Man; they were two of a kind. He told me that we were an imposition, he did not want us there, we were forced on him and there were no enemy combatants anywhere around his sector of responsibility.

We would be expected to assist in daily chores, he said. "One of your men will pull KP each day," he stated with all of the authority a lieutenant fresh out of Officer Candidate School could muster. He had forty men eating in his mess tent, I had four. Yet he still expected us to carry an equal load.

It took four men to run the lights. We had five men so that each night a man would have a night off.

I explained that we worked nights and needed to sleep during the day. Somehow this was a foreign concept to him: searchlights are useless in the daytime. We agreed to disagree. In exchange for not pulling KP, we would eat C-Rations and not use his mess tent. In exchange for using his latrines (holes in the ground), we would assume nightly guard duty, relieving four of his men.

C-Rations

C-Rations were combat rations and were designed to provide the nutrition a warrior would need in the field. They would survive in any temperature and under the most stringent conditions. They would offer a variety of options and they would never go bad. They were amazing. When we first arrived in Nam the "rats" were over ten years old; when we left they were fresher since the reserves of C-Rats had been exhausted and production of C-Rations had been accelerated.

The Army uses three colors in their design palette: olive drab (OD), dirt brown and black. C-Rats were packed twelve to a case. A C-Ration box, dirt brown, contains some tin cans, OD in color, and other packaging. The primary contents of each meal are noted on the outside of the box in black ink. A small can opener, about half the size of a quarter, OD in color, was used to open the cans.

My favorite meal was "BEEFSTEAK WITH POTATOES AND GRAVY" and my least favorite was "HAM WITH LIMA BEANS". A dessert was included in each meal. The one stolen most often was fruit cocktail; the one stolen least often was fruit cake.

Once a month, those of us on a steady diet of C's would receive a "Sundry Pack" which contained soap, razor blades, cigarettes, matches and chocolate candy among other items. The chocolate candy was formulated so that it would not melt in the tropical heat. It would, however, go through the digestive system in record time so we stayed away from it.

Whenever we drove the jeeps back to base camp there would be children on the sides of the road yelling, "Gimme chop-chop, GI!" On one trip to the rear we decided to toss the chocolate candy to the kids. On the way back to the hill hours later, those kids were squatting in rice paddies, flipping us the bird and yelling, "You number ten, GI!" Number ten was the worst someone could be. Such ingratitude.

Figuring It Out

Since we were one of the first units deployed we would figure out what worked and what didn't with the searchlights.

One rainy night the clouds were low and visibility was poor. We were asked to sweep a river about a half mile from Hill 327. The light was powerful enough to reach there so the Marine who had requested help got on our frequency. At his direction we swept the river back and forth.

While we were doing this we saw tracers coming in our direction from the other side of the river, another half-mile from where we were sweeping.

The next day we would learn that the shooters were Marines shooting at us because we had inadvertently illuminated their motor pool. The light was so intense that it bounced off of the river, went up and bounced off of the clouds and still had enough oomph to illuminate a friendly position. I made sure the folks at base camp got this information.

One night we were running a mission using infrared and Martin, one of my crewmen, saw a Viet Cong walking along the wire about twenty feet in front of us. The noise of the jeep's engine did not deter him – he knew he was safe. This was a no-fire zone so we could not shoot at him.

The next morning we reported the sighting to the Marine lieutenant but he did not believe us. I reported it to my platoon sergeant, Sgt. Dawkins, and he passed the message to our lieutenant. The reply was I should not make waves.

A couple of nights later Charlie was back with a friend. I watched the green fuzzy image in the infrared binoculars and radioed for permission to fire. Yes, we had to ask; there are rules in conventional warfare. Before anyone could answer, Charlie was gone. It would not have mattered if they had gotten back to me quickly since the order was to stand down.

Several more sightings were similarly ignored and my protestations resulted in us being removed from Hill 327. Since my men had seen and verified the sightings as well, they were ready to leave. Another team from our battery would take our place and the Marine lieutenant would repeat his assessment that there were no Viet Cong in his sector.

Back in base camp our platoon commander who reported to the Old Man pulled me aside and said he understood. I think he did. He was one of the officers who "got it"; he believed that there really were enemies in the area. After all, what else could explain the body bags we saw from time to time?

Then he pulled out a map, pointed to Hill 55 and told me to take my men there. We were to drive the forty minutes out to the hill and it was already late afternoon.

The Americans owned the daylight hours and the Viet Cong owned the nights. That is why the searchlight experiment was initiated. We were a part of a bastard unit someone in the Pentagon put together to change the night into day and take away the advantage the enemy had of being able to use the darkness. The concept looked good on paper, I'm sure.

Everything was packed in the jeeps, and the trailers. Since the searchlight took all of the space in the back of the jeep, there were only two seats in each vehicle. There were five of us. One man had to fold himself into the back of a jeep and wedge himself in by the light for an uncomfortable, long ride. This was against regulations but it was the way we had been trained. Once again, the old regulations had not yet caught up with the new Army.

The roads were not really roads. There were only a few that had gravel and even fewer with pavement; most were simply dirt trails. The dust from the roads would cover us and fill our rifles.

Using the map, my driver, Martin, and I led the other jeep to Hill 55. We had never been out that way and were not sure we could find the hill. But, orders are orders so we went and we needed to arrive before dark.

I was told to find the Marine supply sergeant on Hill 55 and draw C-Rations for five men for five days. I assumed this had been arranged. I was wrong. It was dark when we arrived at the remote encampment and when I gave the Marine supply sergeant my request he responded by saying, "You're Army, aren't you?" There is no love lost between the Doggies and the Jarheads. Then he asked, "Can you get us some rations? We have a real problem with resupply."

That was the night I began my life of "crime". Hill 55 is where I would stay for the next ten months. We learned that to have whatever we wanted or needed, we would have to take a page from Whittaker' book. The conventional book of warfare the Old Man used would not serve us well on Hill 55. We would prefer the Whittaker way and the Marine way.

THE FEW, THE PROUD, THE MARINES

Any leader would benefit from studying the Marine Corps process for building men into cohesive units.

The Corps is a part of the U.S. Navy and began as the landing force for watercraft. Over time they have suffered from reduced budgets and comments about them being redundant and unnecessary.

There is no higher level of pride than the pride of the Corps.

Several retired Marine officers have emerged as senior executives in my client organizations. When they have discussed this topic they explain that the Marines are the smallest branch and can be more selective in the people they allow in. Their officers tend to be less elite than their counterparts in other branches and are able to interact with their subordinates and still maintain respect and control. It is an enviable and masterful skill.

Today I work primarily with CEOs. When I learn that a potential client was in the Marines, I know I will see the best in leadership.

Never have so few been asked to do so much with so little.

We heard numerous explanations about why the Marines had to use outdated equipment. Most of these revolved around budgets and the fear that if the Marines asked for the money they really needed, the decision would be made to dissolve the Corps.

When the Army retired a piece of equipment it would go to the Army Reserves who would then pass it along to the National Guard who would then pass it to the Marines. That was the story, anyway, and it helped explain why the Corps was occasionally using equipment we had never seen before.

In Vietnam their jeeps were Mighty Mites which were an American Motors substitute for the jeep and was supposedly capable of being dropped from an airplane and still run. The Marine helicopters were Korean War vintage, were two stories tall, noisy and creaky but they flew Marines into the most savage battles.

As a result of our experience being attached to various Marine divisions, I have nothing but respect for those who served in the Marine Corps.

Semper fi.

Our second week on Hill 55 we would be assigned to a position on the north side of the hill. In the early morning hours we would watch as Hill 327, our previous home, was overrun. There were many casualties, including the other team from G Battery of the 29th Field Artillery.

I did not feel exonerated. And, I had dodged another bullet.

## **P.T.S.D.**

*The unreliability of the military leadership was continuing. The difference now was that the outcome was potentially disastrous. Respect for authority was diminishing. While an inept decision at the Pentagon had placed a few of us in leadership positions that we were not trained to manage, inept decisions now led warriors into deadly traps.*

# CHAPTER FIVE

## Hill 55

Almost a half-mile long and two hundred yards wide at the widest point, Hill 55 was a grotesque lump of misshapen dirt completely defoliated by Agent Orange. In retrospect it seems illogical that the hill where the military would encamp would be stripped of all vegetation while the surrounding countryside would be a thick jungle. We would be exposed both to the enemy and to the elements while the enemy could come within grenade throwing range without being seen.

The Marines would call this desolate piece of real estate Hill 55. Since it was 55 meters high, all anyone had to do was to look at a topographical map and find the number "55". The highest elevations were always noted on the map. When the Army took over the hill later in the war, they would call it a firebase.

The bare hill was baked in the sun every day from dawn to dark. The ground was as hard as a clay pot. As tires and feet rubbed the surface, a fine dust would be created and would cover and permeate everything. The dust in our noses affected the way everything smelled and the dust in our mouths flavored everything we ate or drank.

The hill had been occupied at various times by different military units, mostly U.S. Marines. When the Americans first occupied the hill there few enemy troops were around. The hill was basically a secure encampment where infantrymen could find refuge from the jungle. The Viet Cong guerillas would move into the jungle and valley that surrounded the hill. By the time of the TET Offensive a considerable number of North Vietnamese Regulars, the NVA, would be working from the jungle and tunnels surrounding the hill.

As time progressed, some offensive units were added to the hill. A 105 MM artillery battery dug in six cannons, erected a hooch for officers, a tent for enlisted men and a tent for the command center.

The command center would include a Fire Direction Control (FDC) center which was comprised of a radio operator, an artillery specialist who could determine where to point a 105 and how much gun powder to use and an officer to oversee their activities. This officer was known as an FDO, Fire Direction Officer. A Forward Observer (FO), also an officer, would call in the coordinates of a target. The radioman would read the coordinates to the specialist who would plot them on a map. Then, using various calculations, he would determine the direction, known as an azimuth, and an elevation for each 105 that would fire. He would determine which type of projectile would be used and how much gunpowder would be needed to insure the projectile reached its target.

Any miscalculation would result in the artillery round dropping in the wrong place. Too many times this would result in "friendly fire" – Americans killed by Americans.

Using a wired field telephone the specialist would send the information to someone on the gun crew. Assuming the gun crew set the azimuth and elevation correctly, measured the right power and loaded the correct projectile, the FO would see something happen in the general area where he had seen the target.

The FO could adjust the subsequent rounds in "clicks". Initially, a click was supposed to be a kilometer or close to a mile. Because the war was being fought in close quarters, a click was one grid mark on the map. Depending on the unit and their maps, a click could be 100 feet, 100 yards, 1000 feet or 1000 yards. Again, the possibility for error was significant. Adjusting "right two clicks" might cause the next round to be closer to or farther from the intended spot than the FO had wanted.

Most artillery rounds were explosives. They would land, explode and spray shrapnel in all directions. Between the concussion and the flying metal, little would survive unscathed. The initial round, however, might be white phosphorus which would create a large plume of white smoke when it exploded. The FO could use this to adjust subsequent rounds. At night, we would need to see the initial flash of the exploding round since the smoke was difficult to see in the dark.

A rare form of artillery had a timed fuse and would cause the shell to explode in the air spraying shrapnel in all directions. These shells were expensive, hard to come by and rarely used.

Another unit on the hill was an 80MM mortar battery with its own FDC. A mortar is a steal tube resting on a base plate, pointed upwards and supported by a tripod or bipod. A round would be dropped in the tube. When it hit bottom, the firing pin would be engaged and the projectile would head for the sky at an angle. When it landed, it would explode – hopefully near its intended target. The mortars were less accurate but more portable than their big brothers, the 105s.

The gooks had what they called knee mortars because they braced them with their knees instead of a tripod. Essentially it was a tube. They would use mortar rounds seized from American installations they had overrun and guess at where the round would go. Then they would adjust their subsequent rounds. They had no FDC and were often about as accurate as we were.

In the early days of the war before we arrived there were few fire missions for the artillery and mortar batteries on Hill 55 so they invested their time making the hill look more like home.

Our first night on the hill was an unexpected surprise for the Marines. We thought they were expecting us and they thought we knew what we were doing. We hardly knew our capabilities and limitations and the Marines we were supporting did not even know we existed. As often happens in the military, communications had broken down. Communicating within a unit was difficult enough; communicating between an Army unit and a Marine unit was close to impossible and would plague us the entire time I was there.

The officer in charge of the hill pointed to a bunker we would use and then told us to set up on the north side of the hill immediately. We could unpack our gear the next morning but it was getting dark and he wanted to see what we could do.

I glanced in the direction of where he had pointed. The bunker looked like an old, unkempt stack of pillows. The sandbags were bleached white, some were leaking sand from bullet holes and rips from shrapnel. We would check it out in the morning.

During the first night on the hill we set up the lights, ran some missions and gave our new neighbors a look at what we could do.

When the sun came up we drove the jeeps over to the bunker. We were surprised to find that the road leading to the bunker was flanked on both sides by numerous state flags. Everyone on the hill had written home for a flag. As they arrived, some spent artillery casings were welded together to form a long tube. The tubes were partially buried in the ground leaving six feet sticking out above the roadbed and filled with dirt. The flags, secured to posts, were jammed in the dirt in the tubes.

This colorful display seemed out of place on the barren hill, but there it was.

FINGERS

Five ridges protruded from the primary bulge of the hill and were known as fingers. They were numbered beginning at "noon" or as close to north as possible.

Finger one was on the north side where we watched Hill 327 being attacked. Later we would watch the TET offensive begin from that point. Finger one faced towards the DaNang airbase several miles away.

When we first arrived on the hill the area around it was a no fire zone. Anyone who fired a single round would be expected to produce an enemy soldier's body and his weapon. Since this was impossible, we never fired our weapons even when fired upon.

One night I used the infrared binoculars to watch a group of armed men, Viet Cong, walk up to a peasant's hooch. They sat on the porch for a while, smoked some cigarettes and eventually walked away. When I reported the sightings I was told there were no enemy combatants in our sector. The senior commanding officer on Hill 55 at that time, Marine Major Andrews, was the source of this information as well as the one who created the no fire restriction.

Finger two had the main road from the rear across its ridge line. We could see any vehicle heading for the hill for some distance since finger two was fairly long. Later this would help us prepare for the Old Man's surprise visits.

One evening around dusk we saw a Marine Mighty Might, their version of a jeep, making a dust plume coming up on finger two. It was not a good idea for the any Americans to be out of a secure area that late in the day. The gooks would be moving around. That was why we had been timid about our arrival time our first night on the hill.

As it topped the rise of finger two the Mighty Might took fire from both sides of the road. It was an ambush. Before we could lock and load and get permission to fire, the VC had swarmed the vehicle, one body had been dragged away and the other left slumped over the steering wheel.

It turns out that Captain Andrews' best friend, a light colonel, was coming out to the hill to visit. The two friends would spend the night drinking and playing poker. That was the plan.

Since the squad that went out a few minutes later could only retrieve the body of the driver and the vehicle, the light colonel would be listed as an MIA.

That night Captain Andrews lifted the no fire restriction.

Our first party began that night when a 105 recoilless rifle fired a projectile directly into the hooch we had been watching for weeks which happened to be lit up with a searchlight. The VC were there on their nightly visit, squatting down casually and smoking. After all, we had never fired on them before. Tonight would be different.

The resulting firefight only lasted a minute or two; bamboo and grass burn quickly.

Finger three was on the south side of the hill. The jungle hugged closest to the hill at finger three. Charlie could actually sit in the tree line and talk to us without raising his voice. After the no-fire order was lifted we began strafing the tree line with machine gun and rifle fire so Charlie retreated back into the trees. Apparently our new-found courage and willingness to actually shoot back caught him off guard. Charlie would need to develop some new strategies.

He found himself a PA system. He would put a speaker up in a tree and speak into a microphone. We had no idea where he was so we just listened.

One night he began talking to us about personal matters. He called a Marine by name, talked about his girlfriend and called her by name. He referred to the Marine's hometown and even his high school. This was demoralizing and made the war personal.

After that episode it was decided that the locals could no longer come up on the hill and carry away our garbage. We assumed that was where they were getting their intelligence.

Charlie had enough material to carry on his psychological guerilla warfare for a couple of weeks. Though he never mentioned *my* name, I was as adamant about taking him out as anyone.

Charlie apparently did not understand the abilities of infrared detection and he could not contain his curiosity. One night he walked to the tree line, microphone and bullhorn in hand. Two salvos of mortars either took him out, erased his enthusiasm or broke his speaker. Whatever happened, he no longer read bedtime stories to us.

Finger four was only a small knoll that jutted out on the south side and was never used for anything tactical.

Finger five was party central. Most of my nights during my ten months on Hill 55 would be spent on finger five. I would change there, grow up there, earn a medal there and revisit finger five in my mind, day and night, awake and asleep, for many years after returning home.

For all appearances, it was the hill next door. It extended out the west side of the Hill 55. We had to travel down into a ravine and then back up the other side to reach finger five. Since the ravine did not reach the valley floor, this hill was considered a part of Hill 55. It was about two hundred yards away and had its own perimeter of barbed wire and tangle-foot.

The perimeter wire was known as concertina, barbed wire coils about four feet in diameter that had been stretched out and pinned down with traditional barbed wire. The wire holding down the coils was known as tangle-foot because it zigzagged close to the ground. It was designed to slow down anyone on foot. As the enemy tried to navigate through the barbed wire coils, their feet would be tripped by the crisscrossing barbed wire at ground level. It looked menacing. Flares and mines were added to the wire as were tin cans with rocks in them. We wanted to know when anyone was in the wire. "The wire" was our first line of defense.

We had already learned that the wire was not as effective as the military thought. One morning after breakfast when we first arrived in base camp we came out of the mess tent with whatever fruit was available. That day it was apples. A small Vietnamese boy was outside the wire and yelled to us, "Gimme chop-chop GI!" Someone threw an apple but it landed short, right in the middle of the tanglefoot. Without flinching, the kid walked into the tanglefoot, picked up the apple and walked back to his side of the wire. He never even broke his stride.

We realized that tanglefoot, like some of our other defenses, would be pretty much useless.

What functioned as a road between the hill and finger five had gates in the protective wire. So, to make our way from the hill to the finger, the driver would approach the gate, I would get out, open the gate, allow the jeep to pass through and then close the gate on the outside of the perimeter. At that moment we would be in no-man's land.

As we approached finger five there would be another gate and we would repeat the process and find ourselves in the relative security of a small hill in the middle of the jungle, the infamous finger five.

Again, finger five was completely defoliated. The Marines had some above-ground bunkers and a detachment of about twenty men who lived on the finger full time. They would do all they could to make the place feel like home. Pin-up posters were everywhere, short-timer's calendars were around and pictures of girlfriends and cars were used to make the crude place seem less like a war zone.

One Marine had a battery-powered record player and two albums: Johnny Cash's greatest hits were alternated with Petula Clark's.

Finger five had an excellent view of a wooden bridge that spanned a semi-polluted river. The river was important to the locals for irrigation, bathing and, incredibly, drinking. The bridge was important to the Americans for moving around men and materials. Our mission was to protect the bridge.

To confuse the enemy who might be listening in on our radios, we would refer to the bridge as the "Golden Gate" or the "Brooklyn". We would fool ourselves into thinking they would never figure it out.

There were seven bridges on the road from DaNang to An Hoi, a strategic outpost for the Marines. Ours was the only wooden one and ours was the only one still standing when I left Vietnam. Even the elaborate steel bridges we had used on our trips to the rear were bowing their heads into the rivers when I made my last trip to base camp. They had been replaced with pontoon bridges that rocked lazily as we drove across them.

Our humble bridge was about two hundred feet long and in the dry season stood about ten feet above the river. It was a one-lane bridge for military vehicles but the locals had no problem driving both ways across the bridge at the same time. It looked like a game of chicken sometimes but, just as they did on the narrow streets, they navigated around each other with some unknown set of rules.

The banks of the river were thick with trees. The Seabee's, the Navy's construction unit, had made an attempt to clear the vegetation from around the bridge but the jungle undid their work almost immediately. The combination of prolific foliage and an abundant water supply created a thick mass of hiding places for the VC.

On "our" side of the bridge, the side closest to the finger, the Marines had a guard bunker that would accommodate about six men. These men would stand guard and engage with Charlie as he made numerous attempts to drop the bridge into the water. A couple of Marines would walk the bridge all night watching for unusual debris floating in the river as well as unnatural movement in the tree lines.

The other end of the bridge was the beginning of the enemy's turf. The nights belonged to the Viet Cong. After all, that was the reason the Pentagon formed the searchlight units and the reason why we would spend many nights on finger five.

A typical night on finger five would have Martin and me go out at dusk and pass through the two gates. We would keep the jeep below the ridge line so that Charlie could not see where it was. After dark, we would back the jeep into a position where we could see the bridge and use the light as a weapon. Martin would set up the machine gun slightly down the hill behind the jeep and load it with a long bandolier. Then we were ready to party.

We would both have on our flack vests and would have our steel helmets close by. I would uncover and unlock the light so it would be ready to use. Once I had my M16 rifle leaning against the jeep and the M79 grenade launcher loaded and laying on the hood, I would radio the Marine command bunker and tell them we were ready. If there was no command to shoot a mission, I would fix my first cup of instant coffee. Using some semi-clean water and the small Army-issued gas burner, I would hold my canteen cup over the flame until the water steamed and the instant coffee mostly dissolved.

Occasionally we would start the jeep's engine, turn on the light and sweep the area either with the white light or the infrared. And usually we would see nothing of importance.

From time to time the Marines on the bridge would spot something and tell us where it was. Using the infrared I would search it out, find it and then let them know I was about to light it up. As soon as I flicked on the white light everyone would fire into whatever I had illuminated. From the bridge, from our machine gun and from the weapons of the Marines who lived on the finger there would be a shower of various rounds going into the light.

Every fifth round in a machine gun's bandolier is a tracer round. That way the gunner can see where the bullets are going. When everyone was firing into the light all we could see going into it was the tracers. Occasionally we would also see an explosion indicating we had hit something significant of Charlie's and we would cheer.

Charlie figured out that when the light came on the party would start so the light became one of his primary targets. It was a pest that needed eradicating.

For a couple of months we fell into a pattern on finger five. We did our thing and Charlie did his. We lit up his turf, sprayed it with small arms, mortars and, occasionally, artillery. He responded in kind with small arms fire from carbines and AK-47s, mortar rounds and an occasional grenade when the gooks were close enough.

During the firefights, we would be encouraged by Petula Clark. The grunt who had the record player would turn it on and up to full volume when the firefight began. During lulls in the action we could hear her. Then, during clean up after the party which might include body bags and busy corpsmen and medevac helicopters the dirty deeds would be accomplished while she sang, "Don't Sleep in the Subway, Darling."

It was one of many strange juxtapositions: part hell, part home.

Then things changed. The Marine unit assigned to the hill was sent to the DMZ and another unit took their place. The new unit arrived late in the afternoon and did not have time for a briefing before dark. They camped on the hill and did not occupy finger five but still expected us to go out and guard the bridge. We barely had time to find what radio frequency they were using so we could communicate that night. Martin and I would accompany a squad of grunts for their first experience on the finger.

Charlie popped a few rounds in our direction and we cautioned the Marines not to return fire. The VC knew a new unit was on the hill and they wanted us to fire back so they could see what weapons the new unit was using. Trying to outthink the enemy, often by thinking like them, was a game played in our heads that would contribute to the inevitable PTSD.

It did not take long for Charlie to capitalize on the change.

The following morning we returned to the hill from finger five as usual at sunup. Around ten that morning while we were sleeping, a new 2nd lieutenant and a squad of grunts went out to finger five to check it out in the daylight. The bunkers left behind by the previous Marine unit had already been booby-trapped and the new unit took its first casualties. Somehow the gooks had managed to go up on the finger in broad daylight between the time we left at dawn and ten that morning and set their traps without being seen.

A demolition team was sent to find and detonate the remaining explosives. Once completed, a tank with a bulldozer blade on the front went out and destroyed the bunkers. Everything on finger five was leveled leaving a bald, rugged dome in the middle of the jungle.

From then on, we would go out on the finger before dark to look for traps and we would be accompanied by the blade tank and a squad of grunts. For the next nine months the Army search-light crew and the Marine tank crew would become as close as anyone could in a war zone where we made it a habit not to know anyone too well.

The blade tank proved to be a useful machine. The tank commander, TC, used the blade to dig several slots where we could back in the jeep. This would provide easy cover for the vehicle and quick movement for us.

The blade would also help on an occasion when the Old Man came out on one of his surprise inspections.

My morning sit reps (situation reports) indicated that we were having regular parties and needed a resupply of ammo on a frequent basis. Since the Old Man did not believe there were any VC in our area, he came out to investigate. I learned later he wanted to punish us and considered court martialing me for firing on civilians. After all, in his mind there were no VC in the area. If we had fired our weapons we must have been shooting at civilians. However, he met with the senior Marine officer and heard only good things about how we had been supporting the Marines.

Miffed, he had his driver take him out to finger five to see where the parties had been held. He still did not believe there were enemies in our sector or he would have realized what a fool-hardy activity this was. He and his driver were totally exposed to any half-wit sniper who might have been around.

I will admit finger five was a mess. We saw little need in cleaning up a defoliated hill in a god-forsaken jungle in South Vietnam after a fire fight. There was trash from C-Rations, ciga-rette butts and thousands of empty cartridges from the various weapons.

We were asleep that morning when all of this happened. I was awakened by the Old Man's driver, a real brown-noser, who also managed to wake up Martin and Davis. We needed sleep. After all, we were entertaining Charlie almost every night and were experiencing the dark side of war. Still, he felt the need to yell, "Captain Hayworth wants to see you right now!"

I pulled on my fatigue pants and in that sleepy fog that accompanies too-short sleep, climbed up out of the bunker barefooted.

I took a severe dressing down for being out of uniform and was told we were to pick up all of the expended cartridges and trash on finger five. As I was able to grasp what he was talking about he told me he would be back out to inspect the finger to insure his orders were followed.

Then he said, "The enemy can use the brass (from the expended cartridges) to make weapons."

Here was a captain who lived in the rear, wore a starched uniform, ate hot meals in the officer's mess, entertained himself in the Officer's Club and did not believe there were any enemy soldiers in our sector telling me to keep the non-existent enemy from picking up our brass cartridges and using them against us.

I went back to the rack but by then it was too hot to sleep.

That night I told the tank crew about the captain's visit. Everywhere we walked on the finger we stepped on brass. After all, Martin might spray one or two thousand rounds during a firefight and each of those cartridges would land somewhere. Our M16s would spit out another two hundred or so and there would be a few of the expended shells from the grenade launcher. As impressive as that was, it was nothing compared to the brass around

95

the tank. Two machine guns and large, 90MM canon cartridges were souvenirs of their contribution to the parties.

We sat on the tank and looked at the situation. There was no small amount of garbage mixed in, mostly C-Ration waste.

The tank driver, Donk (short for donkey – don't ask), said, "I got this," and started the twelve-cylinder diesel engine.

With the rest of us sitting on the beast, he began a tank ballet. Moving gracefully – well, gracefully for a tank – and skillfully lifting and lowering the blade, he managed to bury everything in a matter of minutes. He nosed the tank back into position overlooking the bridge, killed the engine and lit a cigarette. It was as if he had just emptied an ash tray – no big deal.

The blade was not always a blessing.

One evening the tank was waiting for us when we arrived at the finger. We noticed a tent had been pitched behind it. Apparently the tank and crew had taken up residence on finger five which made no sense. As we approached their position we understood why.

The stench was unbearable.

I had smelled it once before when we were digging a foxhole back in base camp. Some American bases were built on top of cemeteries to keep the VC from tunneling under our camps. This was a violation of the Geneva Convention, of course, but who cared? All of the grave markers had been removed so we could not know where the graves were or how fresh they might be.

With our three-foot shovels we dug into a fairly recent grave. As soon as we saw what was on our shovels and smelled the odor, we began throwing dirt back into the hole. Washing the shovels did no good so we poured gasoline on them and lit them. That took care of one smell and left us with one that was marginally more pleasant.

The blade tank had been called out that morning to a former rice paddy on the other side of the bridge. Someone suspected that the Viet Cong had buried some of their casualties there. It was important to know how many. So the tank made passes over the field taking a few inches off of the ground with each pass.

Someone was right. However, just revealing the presence of the graveyard was not enough. The tank was ordered to make repeated passes to make sure each body was uncovered and counted. As the odor rose it was mixed with the smell of vomit from most of the people standing around and diesel exhaust. These were hardened Marines but the sight, sound and smell was too much for many of them.

The tank returned to Hill 55 in the early afternoon and went to the tank battery where they shared maintenance and fuel with two other tanks. The battery was evacuated immediately and hurriedly because of the odor. The blade tank crew used a high pressure hose and river water to try and clean the smelly blade. They tried every chemical they could find but nothing worked. They tried burning the blade with diesel but the odor was still repulsive. The debris was embedded in the blade and in the tank's tracks.

They were ordered to go as far away as they could so that put them on finger five. After a few days the smell either dissipated or we got used to it. So each night we would stop noticing it after a few minutes. However, when we returned to our bunker for our morning rest we had to leave our clothes outside.

Eventually the tank was allowed to rejoin society on Hill 55.

## The Bunker

Before arriving on Hill 55 we had already learned that when the Marines got rid of something it was not worth having. We were given a three-man bunker for the five of us. With three cots set up in the bunker there was barely enough room to walk around or to dress. I asked the supply sergeant if there were additional sleeping quarters available. He said there was but it was in a tent, not a bunker, and it was occupied by "brothers".

Some of the myths about combat include the adage, "There are no atheists in foxholes." There are. Men will curse God with their dying breath. Another is that there are no racial or religious prejudices in combat. That is not true either.

Smith and Roberts were black. I had to find sleeping quarters for two of my men and the only space available was in a brother's tent. This would be one of the easiest decisions I would make.

The brothers were militant. They had been drafted or, like Martin, offered the Army as an alternative to prison. Back home, which we called The World, they had been dealt a lousy hand. Now they were stuck in South Vietnam not knowing if they would live to see the next sunrise, eating C-Rations instead of Momma's cooking, suffering heat that made the Deep South seem comfortable and, for some reason, they had an attitude.

The first night we took the jeeps out to the perimeter and showed the Marines what our capabilities were. We stayed up all night and then three of us went to the bunker and two to the tent to unload our gear.

In the early morning hours the bunker was a sad sight and the tent was probably no more attractive. We were too tired to care.

The bunker had been built years earlier. The construction of a bunker was simple. A hole would be dug in the ground about four feet deep. Twelve-inch by twelve-inch wooden columns seven feet high would be placed in the four corners. Two-inch by twelve-inch boards would be nailed to the columns creating a wooden box in the ground that extended three feet above ground level. The same wooden boards would be used to create a floor and roof.

Our bunker had windows for ventilation, thirty-inch by thirty-inch openings on the west and east sides. The valley was on the north side of the bunker so the windows were on the east and west sides to prevent the enemy from shooting directly into the bunker.

An opening to be used as a door was on the uphill side of the bunker. Since the enemy would attack from the downhill side, this would allow us to exit the bunker without being exposed to enemy fire.

The exterior walls and the roof were covered in sandbags which were beginning to leak after being subjected to the elements and ordinance for so long.

Three of us would spend our first night in the bunker and learn why the Marines did not want it..

On the west side of the bunker, about fifteen feet from our window, was the latrine. By Vietnam standards it was average; by Marine standards it was luxurious. Some previous unit that had been on the hill built a four-hole latrine. Not only did it have multiple holes, it also had a four-foot modesty wall.

The latrine system was simple. Positioned under each hole was a half of a fifty-five gallon steel drum. Waste would fall into the drum and once a day the drum would be dragged out where diesel fuel would be added and ignited. Over a period of several hours more diesel fuel would be added until the contents were burned away.

As you might imagine, the odor was repulsive.

The only place the drums from our luxury latrine could be burned was on the west side of our bunker. The wind blew west to east. After hitting the rack at seven AM, the gentle aroma of burning shit would fill our bunker around ten in the morning. We learned to sleep through it.

We stayed in the bunker despite the lack of comforts because it was the lesser of several evils. Besides, later we would find a way to make it home.

One morning I woke up with a pain in my little finger. I looked over and saw a rat the size of a house cat gnawing on my finger tip. He ran away as soon as I moved but he had answered my question about what kind of critter would eat Tupperware to get to my mother's cookies. Without telling her why, I encouraged my mother to send homemade goodies in tins. With a loaded ammo box on top, even the most aggressive rat could not rob me of my treats.

I needed Smith and Roberts with us. They were being subjected to some conversations that could cause problems. In the Sixties, race was a difficult subject. In combat everyone depends on everyone else; still there was the occasional "kill whitey" conversation that could only create problems.

The bunker was not the answer – we needed more space. We would need to find a way to add on to our humble housing.

The Army has rules and regulations for everything. Everything. If Whittaker had taught me anything it was that the rules can sometimes work in our favor. Every two weeks we had to drive the jeeps back to base camp to have them serviced. This trip would mean that we got no sleep that day but it had to be done. On our first trip back I went to our supply sergeant and asked about a tent we could use for sleeping.

We did not want a tent since they are unbearably hot in the daytime when we needed to sleep and the canvas would not stop a bullet or shrapnel. I was thinking we could erect it on the uphill side of the bunker away from the valley and maybe the bunker would provide some protection.

The supply sergeant and I got along well. He informed me that we were entitled to half a hooch. The people in the rear did not want us to know this for two reasons: they wanted the building materials for themselves and they did not want to have to bring the materials out to the jungle. I could not blame them.

But we prevailed. Reluctantly a half dozen clean and starched soldiers came out in a deuce and a half truck with some plywood, two-by-fours and galvanized tin roofing. They reluctantly admitted that they were responsible for erecting the half-hooch. Since they were in a place they did not want to be, their construction project went very quickly. In a couple of hours we had an eight foot by twelve foot room attached to our bunker.

The deuce and a half kicked up a lot of dust as it exited off of the hill at top speed.

Smith and Roberts were eager to move in and came over immediately. They never said why and I did not ask. At least now all five of us "Doggies" were under the same roof.

Next we would need to sandbag the exterior of the new sleeping quarters. Sandbags were easy to come by – even the Marines had plenty of them. The problem was they were empty and had to be filled with sand.

If you have ever filled sandbags you know what a dirty, disgusting job it can be. One person holds open the bag while another shovels in the sand. The person holding the bag ends up with sand all over them including places where they did not think sand could lodge. This would need to be done in the hot tropical sun when we should be sleeping.

So, what would Whittaker do?

I approached the Marine supply sergeant and asked for advice. He thought for a minute and said, "Give me two cases of C's." I went down to our stash of C-Rations, took two cases up to him and went to the bunker for a nap.

I was awakened by the sound of thuds outside the bunker. There I met an old papa-san, an elderly Vietnamese man, and what appeared to be his grandson. They were unloading filled sandbags from an oxcart. The old man appeared to be about 100 years old. He gave me a toothless smile, bowed slightly and he and the boy pulled the empty oxcart away.

They stopped at the Marine supply tent and received their payment: half a case of C-Rations. The Marine supply sergeant had taken two cases of C-rations to contract with the old Vietnamese man but had kept a case and a half for himself for his efforts. We didn't care; we had the filled sandbags we needed.

We spent the afternoon stacking and pounding the sandbags. The walls were protected and one layer of sandbags covered the tin roof. The walls were four feet high and had screening from the top of the wall to the roof. We even had a screen door with a pneumatic closer – such luxury!

The smell of fresh plywood was alluring and the cross breeze from the three open sides was too good to pass up.

Two cots fit nicely in the new addition. As senior-ranking man, I moved out of the bunker into the new space. The others could choose among themselves and it was determined that Davis would be my roommate. Smith and Roberts joined Martin in the bunker.

A status symbol for bunkers in Vietnam was having a parachute for a ceiling. As soon as the new addition was on our bunker, Charlie began partying again. I started calling for artillery flares. Some pieces of artillery would shoot a flare the same way they fired explosive shells. The difference was that a timed fuse would cause the projectile to explode in the air, ignite and release a Willie Peter flare on a parachute.

During the party I would adjust the flares based on the wind. When the party was over I would request a couple of flares off to the west. At least one of them would drift over finger five where we could retrieve the attached parachute.

## We Have Power

Spring turned into summer and taught us a new definition of hot. Being from the South I was used to hot humid weather. Martin had seen his fair share in San Antonio. For the others it was a wake-up call. A fan would help, especially in the bunker.

There was electricity on the hill. The command bunker had a small generator for lights and radios but it was not an option.

It was too far away and it would be impossible to tap into their power without being caught.

Strangely, on the east side of the hill next to finger two was a Hawk Missile battery. Hawk missiles were about six feet long and were mounted three to a launcher and there were three launchers. Hawk missiles were used as an antiaircraft defensive weapon. In other words, their mission was to shoot down the Viet Cong aircraft. The Viet Cong did not even have vehicles, let alone airplanes. Apparently there was a military manual somewhere that said we had to have antiaircraft emplacements every few miles, so here they were.

If there was a useless unit in Vietnam, this was it.

The command center for the missiles was a sophisticated box truck. It ran on electricity and powered the launchers so it had a generator. Outside the truck was a radar dish that would be needed to track the Viet Cong aircraft. Radar also uses electricity but with a significant difference. Radar power is 400 cycles instead of the 60 cycles which is the most common.

The two generators were lined up neatly side by side. The Hawk missile crew, having little else to do, kept them in fine running order. They also took the time to pile five foot high dirt berms around them to protect them and to reduce the noise level.

I had a plan. On our next trip to the rear I went to the supply tent and requested 1000 feet of electrical wire, two conductor, exterior, OD in color. The supply sergeant just smiled. "I don't want to know," he said. He told me to come back in a couple of hours. He would have to send someone to the depot.

We pulled at least one trailer with us whenever we went back to base camp. The trailers had canvas covers to protect the contents from the elements and the most common element was dust. We would be resupplying our ammo, grabbing food from the mess hall and making runs to the PX. On this trip, we pulled both trailers. While the jeeps were being serviced by the mechanics, we commandeered a couple of three-quarter-ton trucks and attached the trailers.

Martin and I headed for the Marine mess tent; the others went to the PX. On their list was an electric fan.

We were wearing green uniforms but we were the color of dirt. The roads were covered with a fine, fine dust like talcum powder. After only a mile or two on the road in the jeeps, our weapons and our clothes were caked.

We knew our place. Folks in the rear assumed we were as unclean as we looked so some treated us like lepers. Most stayed as far away as they could from us. It did not dawn on me that sleeping in a shit-smoke breeze and hanging around rotting flesh might create an unpleasant aura. We still had a macho aura because we were seeing combat and they weren't but some of the admiration seemed to be wearing off.

We knew better than to enter the mess tent so we would go in through the back through the dry supply shelter and request what we wanted. There was one Army soldier who was assigned to the mess and he was nice to us. He knew our preferences and usually gave us what we wanted without much discussion. We would ask for two bottles of Tabasco sauce to flavor our C's, some salt and pepper, a can of potato chips, a small quantity of bread that would not mildew in a couple of days and a few other items.

On this day there was only a crusty Marine in the mess tent. His disdain for "Doggies" was apparent. When I requested Tabasco sauce he said, "I'll get a bottle off of one of the tables."

He was going to bless us with one half-empty bottle when we were going through a bottle a week. While he was retrieving one partially-empty bottle, Martin looked at a case of Tabasco sauce on a nearby shelf. I nodded and he took the entire case out to the trailer and hid it under the canvas.

When I asked for salt and pepper, the same thing happened. Martin put a case of salt and a case of pepper in the trailer and the mess sergeant handed us half-used salt and pepper shakers. We repeated this routine several times and included cases of stuff we weren't even sure we wanted. Despite the stinginess of the mess sergeant, this was one of our most successful shopping trips.

When we returned to the supply tent our supply sergeant was gone – intentionally. He did not want to be a part of whatever we were up to. The PFC he had left in charge pointed to a box that had the wire we had requested. It also contained some electrical outlets and connectors we had not thought of. Interesting.

My training in generator maintenance at Fort Belvoir was about to pay off. While I did not have access to the tools we had been issued at Fort Belvoir and there was no by-the-book protocol for our project, we could make this work. I could strip wire with my bayonet and use tools from the jeep's tool kit for the installation. This was going to usher in a new level of luxury for us.

I had to find the other three men and their trailer for the ammo resupply – our trailer was full of groceries and wire. Once we had loaded up we headed back to Hill 55.

That evening before going out to our positions, we opened a #10 can of tuna, a #10 can of mayonnaise and a #10 can of sweet pickles. Using the forks from our mess kits, we would stab a piece of tuna, dip it in the mayo and chase it down with a pickle. When we had eaten all we could we gave the cans to some Marines since the food would not survive the night in the heat.

Each jeep required a two man crew and there were five of us. So each night one of the four men would have a night off. For the next few nights whoever was off would need to spend time digging a trench from the bunker to the Hawk missile generators. The small trench would need to be as out-of-sight as possible. If anyone asked what they were doing they were to say it was for a ground-field antenna. I had never heard of a ground-field antenna but it sounded official.

It only took three nights. So, on the fourth night, I took the night off and dead-lined one of the jeeps. Inoperable or malfunctioning equipment was considered dead-lined and from time to time one of the jeeps would develop a problem. The malfunction this night was that it would take more than one of us to run and bury the wire.

First I wired the bunker with an outlet, wired another outlet in the addition we had added and then snaked the roll of wire to the screen door. After dark we unrolled the wire in the trench and buried it. I was surprised it went as quickly as it did. Our trench stopped at the berm around the generators so we had to dig a few more feet to reach the distribution buss on the side of the 60-cycle generator.

Fortunately the generator was running so no one would hear us. I cut the wire, stripped it and fed it up behind some other wires that apparently ran to the command truck. After opening the cover I saw that the buss had plenty of unused terminals and it was easy to find a place to attach our pipeline to electricity.

There was a problem. The wire I was using did not look like the other wires in the box. It would be obvious to anyone who looked that the last wire on the terminal block would be a rogue connection. I rubbed dirt on our wires and it helped but I was still concerned.

It occurred to me that people might be suspicious if the last wire attached to the terminal block looked different. But they would not suspect anything if it appeared that the wire had been there a while. So, I disconnected the third wire, chosen at random, and moved it to the vacant position I would have used for our connection and then attached our wire at the number three position.

The only thing that could have gone wrong would have been that I might have disconnected something important that would bring a technician out to the generator. Apparently the number three item was not important or noticed for the short time it was disconnected.

Back at the bunker we turned on the fan and sucked in air from the east side and blew it out the west side. In the morning we would no longer enjoy the aroma of burning sewage.

When I laid down that night I stared up at the parachute ceiling and listened to the hum of the electric fan. We had used fans at home in Atlanta so it was a familiar sound. Tomorrow we would dine royally on the goods we had absconded from the Marine mess tent and that now crowded our living quarters. Life was good, I thought.

It wouldn't last.

## **P.T.S.D.**

*How much more traumatic could anything be than to hear the enemy, the people sworn and determined to kill you, reading your mail from home? Meanwhile, there was a daily struggle for surviving the enemy's best efforts and for attaining the basic creature comforts. In this environment, foreign in so many ways, the stress level grew daily and was mostly undetected.*

# CHAPTER SIX
## Station Break 44

S tation Break Four-Four was the call sign for the five Army soldiers that were attached to a Marine unit that was attempting to hold Hill 55 several miles southwest of DaNang. We were green when we arrived on the hill and we were thoroughly seasoned – and scarred - when we left.

The original four members of the team were Martin, Davis, Smith and Roberts.

I was the senior ranking soldier and was responsible for everything that happened to the five of us. I had to find a place for us to live, food for us to eat, and determine what our mission would be each night. All of this was dependent on what we learned and earned from the Marines. Over time we would earn a lot, including their respect. But it would not be easy.

I was also held accountable for the health and conduct of the soldiers based on U.S. Army protocol. This would become increasingly difficult. For a period of time we could not find potable water. We had a five gallon ration of clean water per day for the five of us. I made the decision that each man would have one gallon, about enough for four canteen refills. We had some other water we could use for shaving and bathing but there was some doubt about whether we would be cleaner or nastier for having used it.

This was another time the Old Man chose to write me up. The hygiene of my men was slipping he said. When the first lieutenant brought me the message from the Old Man we suggested that the easiest way to correct it was to have someone from the rear bring us clean water since they had plenty. That would mean leaving the safety of base camp, driving four hours on very dusty roads and, frankly, no one in the rear wanted to do that. So we were spared any discipline or further discussions on the subject of hygiene.

I was a twenty-year-old tee-totaling, non-smoking virgin who did not use profanity when I was drafted. Except for the profanity, these would remain intact. I read my Bible every day and attended chapel services once a month when a chaplain came around. This made me about one hundred and eighty degrees out of phase with almost everyone else around me. My four men were each at a different level of maturity mentally, physically and spiritually. The five of us had trained together at Fort Sill so they knew what I expected from them and I knew their preferences as well.

Their replacements did not. Whenever one of the other four had to be replaced, I would need to quickly bring the newcomer up to speed as much for their own safety as anything else. Occasionally one of the men would go on R&R or go back to the rear for some other purpose and we would have to make do with a replacement.

We had a reputation back in base camp. Since our position was seeing more action that most others, we were viewed as seasoned combatants. When we went back every two weeks to service the jeeps, showing up covered in in dust and sweat and smelling terrible added to the mystique. On a few occasions I had to radio our command bunker instead of the Marine bunker during a firefight. When I did, I would learn later, the troops back in the rear would huddle in the radio bunker and listen to the firefight. I also learned that they were surprised that I did not show up with a cigar in my mouth cursing like a sailor. Stereotypes die hard.

Their first night on the hill the replacement would work with one of the others. I figured that during the night they would learn the real rules of engagement and hear what an offbeat bastard I was. For the next few nights they would go out with me. I would spend the entire night drilling them on how we do things. Unless we were attacked during the night it would be just a training experience.

If any of the replacements had actually volunteered to come out to Hill 55, I was suspicious. Who in their right mind would want to be in a hot combat zone? The answer was people who are immature and those who think they are commandos. I had no time for either.

Some learned; some did not.

One of the replacements, Chumley, stood up during a fire fight and attempted to fire the machine gun from the hip the way Hollywood actors did in the movies. This was despite my insistence that the gun always remained on the ground in the tripod. As he fired, the barrel of the gun naturally rose and pulled to the right. That's what happens when you fire a machine gun from the hip. The Marine tank was off to his right and he managed to spray bullets on the tank. Fortunately the crew was buttoned up inside.

I ran over and kicked him in the small of the back which sent him and the gun sliding down the side of the hill. He went down face first. The firefight continued with no sign of the rookie. There were Claymore mines where he landed and it occurred to me that he might engage with one. But the rest of us were too busy to worry about him.

After the party was over the tank commander and I called in our sit reps. I poured a cup of the worst possible instant coffee and walked over to check on the Marine grunts who were fighting with us. When I returned to the jeep the rookie was just making his way back up the hill. He was a bloody mess from the slide down the hill. After he dressed his wounds he climbed in the jeep and asked if I would put him in for a Purple Heart. I told him to go ask the Marines on the tank who he nearly killed if they thought he deserved a "Purp".

The next day he was returned to the rear for his own safety. The last time I saw him he was pulling KP in the Marine mess tent.

The Marines gave me forward observer status which was usually reserved for officers. A forward observer is someone who spots the enemy's location, calculates the coordinates on a map and sends the coordinates to the rear. Then artillery, mortar, air support or even naval gunfire can be dropped on the enemy using those coordinates. If I had given the wrong coordinates, the ordinance might drop in a vacant area, on civilians or on friendlies.

I was given this responsibility despite the fact that I was not an officer for two reasons: I had been to map-reading training at Fort Sill and we were running short of officers. The ones that remained had no problem letting someone else go out to the point and look for Charlie. Finger five was, most nights, the point anyway.

So here I was, an innocent twenty-year-old with the firepower of my team at my control and access to 60MM and 80MM mortars, 105 artillery as well as 155 self-propelled for a while, the occasional helicopter gunship and, on three occasions, a fighter jet. One night just before the Tet Offensive, I had the support of a U.S. Navy ship whose captain needed some notches on his belt. They were remarkably accurate.

It is still hard for me to imagine a twenty-year-old with that level of authority.

I could also direct the fire of the tank that usually traveled with us. Their 90MM canon, 30 caliber and 50 caliber machine guns would be helpful many times.

The version of me that came home would try to resume the innocence I had when the draft notice came in the mail and I would try to pick up where I left off in the days before Vietnam. That was my plan, anyway.

*** 

The five of us used our last names when referring to each other. Nicknames were used for and by everyone else. The reason was that we really did not want to know someone who might not make it through the next skirmish. When Short Round took a bullet through the neck I did not have to attach to that event the sorrow of what his parents, wife or girlfriend would feel. For all I knew he was an orphan.

The tank commander was Skully which referred to his tattoo. Scab was the loader, Smitty the gunner and Dong the driver.

Short Round was the shortest man among the Marine squad that supported us.

The Marines called me *Eveready*, like the flashlight; Martin was San Antone – he was from San Antonio; Davis was Boone – he was from Kentucky; Smith was Chicago and Roberts was Slim.

MARTIN

Anywhere other than Vietnam our paths would not have crossed. Martin had a rugged face and the traces of a person who had already lived more in his nineteen years than he should have. The deep furrows in his face seemed out of character for a person with a twenty-eight-inch waist. Of course most of us were slim. (After my seasick diet on the troop ship I was down to 135 pounds on my 5' 11' frame and came home at 125.)

Martin always had the appearance of being unkempt. He smoked continuously and talked rarely. When Roberts was replaced by Flores, a Hispanic, he and Martin became close friends which was odd. Martin had shown contempt for non-whites, especially those from Mexico. It turns out that Flores had connections for drugs which they shared so they became best friends and coconspirators. They understood that if I ever saw them using drugs I would have to bust them. I understood that everyone had a loaded rifle and busting them might be my last act as a soldier.

The judge had given Martin the option of going to prison or going in the Army. He never talked about the crime except to say that he didn't do it.

Back at Fort Sill we had packed up all of our gear to be shipped to Vietnam. With nothing for us to do, the Army gave us two week's leave to go home prior to shipping out. Martin went home to a house party where he stayed for the entire two weeks. He left the party to return to the fort. He never mentioned spending any time with his family and I knew better than to ask.

One night in Nam he told me the story. During the house party a man had walked in, pointed a gun at the head of another party goer and said, "In three seconds you'll be dead," and pulled the trigger. Martin was telling me how things were done in his world.

"What happened next?" I asked.

"They drug him outside."

In his world, getting the body out of the house was the end of the story. His disregard for the value of human life was not something I had encountered before. Nor was it something I could condone. But later it would prove to be valuable and, regrettably, a part of my nature as well.

Martin would be the one to replace me when I rotated out and went home. The rule was that the last month we were in country we would go back to the rear. I was due to be discharged from the Army during my eleventh month in-country so Martin would take over the unit for a few weeks and groom his replacement.

Most nights I took Martin out with me. We went to the hottest spot around Hill 55, finger five. We were figuring out how to fight with a searchlight since most of what we had been taught at Fort Sill wasn't working out. The Army can actually be a ready-fire-aim organization sometimes. Our routine became something of a model and others copied it – much to the Old Man's chagrin.

Most nights Martin would drive us out to the finger. We were two very young men each with an M16 rifle and 20 clips loaded with eighteen rounds each. Martin also had the M60 machine gun and 2, 400 rounds of ammunition. I also had the M79 grenade launcher with 24 rounds. We had a stash of hand grenades: a few fragmentary grenades, the kind you see in the movies, and a few white phosphorous, "Willie Peter", to light up a small area. And, of course, we had the searchlight and the radio.

We would go out at sundown to make it as difficult as possible for Charlie to see us and we would return at sunup. Once on the finger we would join up with a Marine tank and a squad of Marine riflemen, grunts, riding on the tank's fenders. After dark he would nudge the jeep into one of the dugouts, set up the machine gun and light a cigarette.

He came up with the idea of setting up dirt-filled wooden ammo boxes to protect us from mortar rounds that landed in front of us and rocket-propelled grenades, RPGs.

Whenever a party started, Martin would jump in the driver's side of the jeep, start it and set the manual throttle so the alternator on the engine could power the light. Then he would slide down to the machine gun.

When the party was over, we would sit and talk – as much as Martin ever talked – with each other, with the tank crew and with the grunts.

Martin had the respect of the Marines. Meanness shows and being mean is an admirable trait in guerilla warfare.

A machine gun is designed to lay down a blanket of fire to cause the enemy to retreat or at least take cover. Martin was not content with that. Every fifth round on a machine gun bandolier is a tracer so the gunner can see where his bullets are going.

Martin made a bandolier of tracers so that every round he fired could be seen. He used it to meticulously adjust the complex sights on the M60 so that he could hit a target more than a hundred yards away with the first round. His ability to use the machine gun as a sniper weapon earned him some extra cash. Whenever a new guy would come out with the grunts, Martin would bet them he could hit a certain tree on the other side of the river on the first shot. He usually won.

One night there was a particularly hot party. The enemy was relentless. I was running the light and acting as a forward observer; Martin and his machine gun were going non-stop.

Machine gun barrels get hot – red hot – and have to be changed out or they will actually droop. Martin had two barrels and an asbestos glove for changing the barrels. In this case, he did not stop to change barrels and the gun jammed.

The light had been taken out but the radio still worked so I was busy. The tank began moving which was not a good sign. They were our first line of defense. We were taking fire from the direction of our secondary positions so the tank was going there and we would need to follow.

I yelled at Martin who was desperately trying to unjam the gun and I pointed to the moving tank. He nodded, grabbed the machine gun and what was left of the ammo and ran to the secondary position as I drove the jeep over to it.

At sunup Martin showed me that he had severely burned his hands on the gun. I told him we would find a corpsman and send him to the rear, if necessary. Then I told him I would put him in for a Purple Heart. That's when he threatened to kill me.

He wanted no record of his hands being burned. Later he would explain why. "New fingerprints," he said.


DAVIS

Davis was the level-headed one of the team. Always calm and always clean. Nothing seemed to rile him. Rather than complain about anything, he would simply find a way to fix it or work around it. He seemed to live with a short-timer's attitude.

He was the same age as I was and found the military's ways of doing things something like a gnat. It would aggravate for a while and then go away. He was another quiet one so I did not know what he was thinking most of the time.

In combat he was steady. He was not a risk taker and seemed to want to make every effort count.

He and I went together on Operation Arizona. We would be out for over a week moving from place to place as the Marines attempted to push a North Vietnamese Army, NVA, unit back to wherever they had come from. Davis would be the driver and machine gunner.

This would be my chance to get to know him well since we would be together 24/7 for several days. If he was ever flustered or out of sorts, I never saw it. He had many opportunities to lose his cool, calm façade but he never did.

While on Operation Arizona, at one point we were joined by a squad of South Vietnamese grunts. The locals were not seen as fearless warriors and some, we had heard, had turned on their American counterparts during firefights. We did not trust them.

Davis and I had dug a hole behind the machine gun so he could stand and fire. The shovel on the side of the jeep and the soft jungle earth made this a fairly easy task.

In broad daylight we spotted a number of Viet Cong walking along the bank on the other side of the river we were flanking. There was no need for the searchlight so Davis instinctively lunged for the hole behind the gun only to find it filled with South Vietnamese soldiers – and others trying to get in.

Davis crouched down and began pulling them out by their collars one at a time, cursing the whole time. By the time he got behind the gun the VC were gone.

I began to wonder if I should not set him up to take over the unit when I rotated back to the States. Martin's hot head and history and drug use were red flags. Finally I concluded that Davis was not mean enough to call the difficult shots. In retrospect, I ws probably wrong.


## SMITH

Imagine the coolest, uneducated African-American from Chicago's south side and you would see Smith. He was too much of a lady's man to be in a gang and too smart to be a criminal. To hear him talk you might think him to be the toughest kid on the block but to watch him in action you would learn that he was as scared as any of us.

He had an easy laugh, a cool strut when he walked and made every attempt to make an Army uniform look urban chic. In the States he would be told to turn his cap straight and to tuck in his shirttail. On Hill 55 I had better things to do than critique Smith's uniform.

Some soldiers bragged about how bravely and courageously they would act when we got to Nam. Once we left the troop ship most of them quieted their bragging. Smith was not one of them; he bragged continuously. His initial introduction to the consequences of war did nothing to change his patter. A truck load of body bags, warnings from men who had been in-country for nearly a year and a body burned beyond recognition failed to dilute his enthusiasm for pending combat.

The morning after his first party would be the beginning of the silencing of Private Smith when the discussion of combat came up. He and Roberts were covering a position on finger 3. We had had a few small parties there before and I felt confident letting the two of them cover the position. I was actually grooming Roberts for a promotion and wanted to see how well he could handle Smith who was his best friend on the hill.

Roberts would relate the incident to us all the following morning to a well-entertained audience and to Smith's embarrassment. It turned out that Charlie popped a few rounds in their direction. Their training would require the following: both men would have on their flack vests with their M16 rifle and their steel helmet nearby. When the party started Smith would start the jeep, adjust the throttle and lay down behind the jeep to fire wherever Roberts pointed the light. Roberts would put on the headset connected to the radio, stand on the right side of the jeep and prepare to shine the light where he was directed.

Roberts did his job by the book. That's when he realized the jeep's engine wasn't running and the light would not come on. When he ran around to the driver's side to start the engine, he assumed Smith had been hit. Instead he heard a voice coming from a trench.

"Roberts! Throw me my vest! Throw me my helmet! Throw me my rifle!"

Not only had he ignored all of his training and violated protocol, he had done so from a trench below ground where neither Charlie nor Roberts could see him.

Afterwards he became a model and courageous soldier. Over time he would begin to return fire even in the hottest situations.

ROBERTS

PFC Roberts was from the Midwest with ingrained mid-west values. He was as street-smart as Smith, fit, capable and could easily handle anything anyone would want to throw at him. And, he went to great lengths to make sure no one knew it. His idea of becoming a veteran was to ride out his two years by doing as little as possible and making no waves.

No one understood the game better than Roberts.

When the Old Man came out to the hill for a surprise in inspection, it was one of Roberts's friends back in the rear who tipped us off. Knowing that there was no way we could clean up Smith well enough to meet the Old Man's standards, Roberts took control. He pulled the canvas cover off of one of the jeep trailers and spread it on the ground. Then he took apart the machine gun, spread the parts out in order on the tarp, found a toothbrush and told Smith to sit across from him. When the Old Man arrived Roberts and Smith were "cleaning" the machine gun better than it had ever been cleaned.

I gave Roberts the night off.

Whenever Roberts was missing I figured something good was about to happen. "Where ya' been?" was answered by a toothy grin. Later we would find a girly magazine or a fresh deck of cards in the bunker.

Over time the team would change for one reason or another. When the platoon commander, the lieutenant, told me I needed to rotate one of my men, I asked where they would go. The bad news was that they would go to a unit closer to the Demilitarized Zone, DMZ, than we were. It was a hot zone, hotter than Hill 55. The good news was that after a few weeks they would be promoted to Corporal. This would make Roberts an E-4 if I sent him, would increase his pay and would allow him to send more money home to the family he discussed rarely but fondly.

When I brought up the topic that someone needed to rotate and explained the whole deal, I thought I saw Roberts smile so he got the job.

The truck that brought his replacement took him back to base camp and he began his journey to the new unit.

He would "buy the farm" a short time later and before getting his promotion. I could only imagine what his family would go through. I felt responsible and decided to put it out of my mind entirely – as I would many other events.

Once stateside I would learn the lesson other veterans would learn. The events do not go out of our minds, they burrow deep inside.

## P.T.S.D.

*Survival in a hostile environment like a combat zone creates its own traumatic stress levels. Realizing that some of the decisions we have made have impacted the lives of others in a negative way has a permanent impact. To keep from becoming a useless basket case mentally, our only alternative was to stuff down the emotion and try not to think about it. We hoped those events would not surface later. (We were wrong.)*

# CHAPTER SEVEN
## Unmet Expectations

Hill 55 Month One/300 Days To Go

**A** soldier has certain expectations in combat.

In basic training we were told that the Army only has the obligation to give us one meal and three hours of sleep each day. Day in and day out we received three square meals a day and the opportunity for eight hours of sleep when we were stateside. So that became our expectation.

Going into Vietnam we realized that being in a combat unit in a combat zone and fighting with a nighttime-only weapon, our meals and sleep would not follow a traditional pattern. We were prepared for that; we were not prepared for some of the other unmet expectations.

Combat soldiers expect that a fully loaded and cocked rifle will perform a certain way: when the trigger is squeezed a projectile will exit the business end of the weapon at a significant enough velocity to achieve the soldier's objective. That would not turn out to be the case with the M16 in Vietnam.

The American military had divided South Vietnam into sections known as corps. The northernmost section stretched from the demilitarized zone, DMZ, that separated North and South Vietnam and extended to a line south of DaNang. This northern area was known as I corps, as in the Roman numeral for one. I Corp was initially held by the Marines and that was the case when we were there as one of the rare Army units in the area.

We were also one of the few units in I Corp to be using the new M16, Black Death, rifle. Once ammo for the M16s was readily available we thought we were set – and we were wrong.

We began hearing stories from other Army units in the southernmost areas of South Vietnam, mostly around the Mekong Delta in IV Corp, that the guns were jamming. Since the Army, not the Marines, were the first to use the M16 in Nam, we relied on the sketchy information from the units in other areas. Army units had been wiped out, we were told, even though their rifles were loaded. It turned out that the weapons in those situations were jammed and inoperative.

This was not reassuring, as you might imagine. For a while the military considered replacing the new weapon with the older M14s – at least they were reliable.

It began happening to us. I would raise the M16 to my shoulder, take aim and pull the trigger and the weapon would work just fine even though it acted peculiarly. When I tried to fire a second round, nothing happened. The cartridge from the first round would be jammed in the breach.

We learned to keep our cleaning rods handy.

The cleaning rod for the M16 was several eight-inch sections of steel rods that could be screwed together to form one longer rod. Once assembled, one end had a folding tee handle and the other end had a slot that a cleaning pad could be passed through. With the cleaning pad in the slot, the rod could be pushed down the barrel and pulled back out using the handle and any debris in the rifle could be removed. Without the pad on it, it was just a straight rod and that's what we needed.

When the gun jammed, we would make sure the bolt was pulled all the way back, grab a cleaning rod and quickly jam it down the barrel. The cartridge that was stuck in the breach would pop out. We could then release the bolt, cock the weapon again and it would be ready to fire.

Here we were with the latest high tech rifle and, in the middle of a firefight, we were jamming a rod down the barrel the same way the soldiers did in the Revolutionary War!

This issue became a high priority for the military for obvious reasons.

The windshield on a jeep will fold down easily and can be removed entirely and quickly by two men. There were two hinges that held the windshield in place and the hinge pins could be easily removed to facilitate removing the windshield. A metal chain was attached to each hinge pin to keep them from being lost. When the pin was in place, as it always was for us, the chain made a perfect loop for us to use for our assembled cleaning rods. We would stand up the rod in the loop an let it rest on a sandbag on the floorboard. When we needed it, it would readily available and easily returned to the loop.

Somewhere back in the rear there was an arms specialist who insisted that there was nothing wrong with the M16. This would mean that he had no intention of finding a fix for the problem since he did not think there was one. He was told about the problems we were having on Hill 55, finger five, and came out to observe first hand and figure out what we were doing wrong.

Apparently when he arrived on the hill he went to the command bunker to check in and then walked down to our bunker and introduced himself. He looked like trouble.

His crisp M16 was on his shoulder with a strap that looked brand new – no smudges, no fraying. He was wearing a starched uniform and shined jungle boots. *Who shines their jungle boots?* I thought. On his other shoulder was a canvas bag with his paraphernalia in it – we had no idea what that would be.

He was all business. "There is no evidence that the M16 is flawed; I'm here to see what's going on." That was his howdy-do. I thought some dead soldiers would be evidence enough but apparently it was not convincing enough for him.

He continued. "First of all, your weapons have to be clean. If they aren't that could cause them to jam." *Oh, my gosh. Clean our rifles? Why didn't we think of that?* Oh yeah, we did. Every single day. In fact the weapons were already showing wear from our frequent cleanings.

He asked to check our rifles and was disappointed to find them to be acceptably clean. "Are all six of your clips loaded with twenty rounds each?" The regulations called for each of us to carry six clips.

"I have twelve clips," I answered, "eighteen rounds each."

"A clip will hold twenty rounds."

"Yes, we know that. However, with twenty rounds in the clip the top bullet can too easily slip forward and the clip won't load.

It sometimes malfunctions with nineteen rounds so, to be on the safe side, we load our clips with eighteen rounds."

"That's not true."

We were not off to a great start and it got worse when he needed a ride out to finger five. The jeeps had two seats so he would have to fold himself into the back. However, Martin and I also carried the M60 machine gun with ammo boxes for 2400 rounds, the M79 grenade launcher with a case of 24 grenades, a handful of frag and Willie Peter grenades and our food. There was not much room left for him in the jeep.

By the time we got to the wire a few minutes later he was whining with discomfort and, even though he was not a Marine, we waited for the Marine tank and let him hop a ride on the tank's fender.

Once on finger five we set up as usual. The searchlight jeep was backed up to a berm and I would back it up on top of the berm once it was dark and Charlie couldn't see what we were doing. Martin had set up the machine gun and placed the canvas cover that normally protected the light on top of the gun. A bandolier of rounds was at the ready; all he would need to do is cock the weapon and pull the trigger.

Ten yards to our right was the Marine tank. It too was at the ready. The guns were unlocked and the loader had three rounds of different types ready to load depending on what type of party we would be having.

As we set up, the arms specialist laid out a tarp he could lay down on and not get his uniform dirty. His M16 was prominently displayed along with six clips holding twenty rounds each. He also had some binoculars, some tools we did not recognize and a single box of C-Rations. He would tell us later that this was his first C-Rat meal.

Martin pulled me aside. "What if we don't get hit tonight?" He cut his eyes over to the specialist. "Will he come back?" Martin did not like having unseasoned, green troops around.

"Don't know. Probably."

We explained to the specialist where the fire would most likely come from and then as the night wore on he asked about our experiences. The fact that we had "war stories" to tell seemed to soften him a bit but did not make him any more popular with Martin.

Sometime in the wee hours a party started. We took some incoming small arms fire. Martin started the jeep and slid behind the machine gun and at the same time the mighty diesel engine on the tank sprang to life.

It was not a long party, probably a few VC who had found a good hiding place with a clear view of finger five who thought maybe they could accomplish something. Like most firefights this one was noisy but the tank could only fire its machine guns since the enemy was too close to the bridge for the cannon to be used.

I had the light on what I thought was Charlie's position. Folks were filling the area with small arms fire. I felt a tap on my shoulder.

It was the M16 specialist asking to borrow my cleaning rod; his gun had jammed.

It turned out that the problem was not the M16 but the particular ammo we were using. M16 rounds from one particular manufacturer would jam because the brass being used was too thin. When the gun was fired the first or second time, it would work fine. However, once the breech got hot and the bullet was fired, the combined heat from the breech and the bullet would cause the brass to expand and jam in the gun.

The extractor would attempt to grab the cartridge and spit it out. Instead, it would merely cut the stuck round and stop.

We never learned how that came to be. Some said the manufacturer was trying to improve their profits by skimping on the brass; others said the specs given to the manufacturer were in error – like a typo. What were we to believe?

Either way, it did not make much difference to the families of the men who died with a loaded but inoperable rifle in their hands.

The specialist rode back to Hill 55 on the tank and we never saw him again. But once we heard about the problem with the bullets we refused to accept ammo from that manufacturer.

ANOTHER UNMET EXPECTATION MONTHS LATER

In the movies we see people pulling the pins out of hand grenades with their teeth. I believe that idea is promoted by the American Dental Association because teeth are more likely to come out than pins when that technique is used.

There is a way to actually do that by straightening out the pin ahead of time but that can cause the pin to come out unexpectedly – not a good thing.

Once the pin is pulled, the grenade is still safe as long as the person holding it keeps the handle, or spoon, in place. Once the spoon is released the grenade will explode in five seconds, just long enough for it to be thrown a safe distance away without the receiving party having time to throw it back.

Because of the density of the jungle, we would sometimes let the spoon fly, count, "one-thousand one, one-thousand two," and throw it with a high arc and then drop to the ground. The idea was that the grenade would explode in the air over the heads of the enemy and inflict more damage than if the shrapnel was buffered by vegetation.

We were instructed not to do that because too many soldiers and Marines were losing their hands and being killed using this practice.

It turns out that it was defective grenades – they had zero-delay fuses. Once the spoons were released the grenades exploded. The warrior did not stand a chance.

Eventually we learned that the fuses in the defective grenades all had the same lot number stamped on the fuse. When we found them we let the folks back in the rear figure out what to do with them.

We considered simply tossing them down the hill where Charlie could find them but then we were afraid that one of our guys would find them so we chose to dispose of them the right way.

This was not a new idea. We were told at the time our aircraft, Marine and Air Force, would drop five-hundred-pound bombs with long-delay fuses on them. The VC would find our unexploded bombs, attempt to disassemble them and use the ordinance against us. They would drag the bomb back to their tunnel or hooch and make their own weapon out of it. The idea was that while they were disassembling them the bombs would explode and destroy the enemy's facility.

It was not an exact science and it was against the Geneva Convention. I think it was just a cover story for the number of bombs that failed to detonate. Unexploded ordinance has been the bane of every modern war long after the wars have ended. Today undetected land mines will harm innocent people in many parts of the world.

We were satisfied that none of our frag grenades had the short fuses but for some reason we had not checked our white phosphorous, Willie Peter, grenades we occasionally used for illumination.

One night Martin climbed out of the jeep saying, "I think I heard something." He grabbed a Willie Peter grenade, pointed to area where we should point our rifles, pulled the pin and let the spoon fly. His intention was to count to three, instead of two, so that the light would be as high as possible when the grenade went off.

The grenade exploded immediately with a familiar and un-mistakable sound. Without thinking, Martin dropped it which was the right thing to do. White phosphorus burns at an incredibly high temperature. Unfortunately, it went directly into the pocket of his jungle fatigue shirt and began burning it way out. With the intensely hot grenade hissing in his pocket, he attempted to step away from it but, of course, his pocket went with him. Then he excitedly jumped and turned all the time swatting his shirt.

It really did not take long for the thing to burn its way out, only a second or two, but it must have seemed longer to Martin.

Once the grenade hit the ground he kicked it as far away as he could and composed himself enough to string together a long and creative string of profanity.

I went back and sat in the jeep to sip on the swill we referred to as coffee. A few minutes later Martin sat in the driver's seat smoking a cigarette. It was one of the few times I would see his hand tremble.

We said nothing to each other.

He was not nursing his hand so I assumed he was okay. He was probably wondering how I was going to react. I was insistent but not a stickler about buttoning pockets. I was more concerned that something we needed would fall out and had not considered the idea that something unwanted might fall in.

We both stared forward through the jeep's windshield. The last wisp of the smoke from the grenade was dissipating.

"I didn't know you could dance," was all I said and the incident was over. Well, except for the smell of burned cloth.

Another Incident Later

During our third month in Nam we finally got jungle fatigues.

On a trip back to the rear to service the jeeps we asked about jungle fatigues. These were uniforms that had been designed for tropical climates and were much more comfortable than the original fatigues we were issued in boot camp over a year ago. The material was significantly lighter, the shirttail was worn on the outside of the pants rather than tucked in and the extra space allowed for large pockets. The pants were also made from the lighter material and had cargo pockets on the legs. Not only were they practical and cool – they made us look better.

Someone had thought through the design and manufacture of this uniform. With the shirttail out, less dirt went down inside our pants. The large outer waist-level pocket on the shirt was handier than we thought so we developed the habit of not buttoning them with the two buttons. The only times that was a problem was when an officer caught us "out of uniform" and the night Martin dropped the illumination grenade.

When we drove into base camp that morning we had seen many of our rear-echelon comrades wearing them so we knew they were available. What hadn't they brought them out to us on a mail run?

Martin was going to the supply tent for resupply of ammo and said he would pick up our new fatigues. This was like Christmas for us.

The supply sergeant was out on R&R and the corporal watching the store was not sure if he was allowed to give us ours even though our names had been sewn on the shirts. Martin never told me what he said or did after hearing the corporal's reply; I just noticed that the corporal loaded the stack of fatigues in the jeep trailer himself.

The searchlights, on the other hand, performed perfectly. The Xenon bulbs lasted the entire time I was there, the mechanisms inside the lights that moved the lens in front of the bulbs only failed occasionally and that was due to dirt that had managed to creep inside the sealed case.

All in all, by the time the military puts something in the hands of a combatant it has been rigorously designed, redesigned and tested. That does not mean it will do what needs to be done in combat.

## <u>P.T.S.D.</u>

*Having abandoned the idea that we could trust our own organization to support us, we were relying on our own strengths. We equated our strength with the quality of the weapons we carried. A machine gun could spray a lot of bullets and an M-16 could accurately take out an enemy warrior. When those, too, began to fail us, each firefight became more traumatic, each day brought more stress.*

# CHAPTER EIGHT
## The First Kill Diet

Hill 55 Month Two/270 Days To Go:

W hat causes us to react as we do when we see a lifeless body?

Perhaps it is a reminder of our mortality, the fact that no one in this life gets out alive.

Most people can go through their lives without ever seeing the body of someone killed by trauma. This is fortunate. Fewer will see the traumatically killed body of someone they actually know. And even fewer will witness the actual trauma that kills someone they know.

For the combatant, this can be a too-frequent occurrence.

Imagine that one morning on your usual route to work traffic is snarled due to an automobile accident. By the time you inch your way up to the scene, you see that a stretcher is being loaded into an ambulance and the body on the stretcher is covered from head to foot. Someone had died in the accident. In a second ambulance the paramedics are stabilizing another victim. You know they are a victim because you can see blood on their clothing. As you pass by you hear the voice of the injured person; screaming, maybe moaning, asking for help.

What happens to you? At least your spirit is disturbed. Your stomach may also react to the experience.

What thoughts go through your mind? What if you had begun your trip to work a few minutes earlier – that could have been you, couldn't it?

Now imagine that this event happens every week. At least once a week you see an accident where people are killed and injured.

Occasionally, the accident happens right in front of you. You hear the noise of the squealing tires and the banging metal on metal contact. You see smoke from the tires and the dust being kicked up by the out-of-control vehicles. You even smell the burned rubber, fuel and other unfamiliar scents.

Would you begin to calculate the odds that perhaps you might be involved in one of these horrible events in the future? Would you begin to look for alternative routes to work?

Now imagine that every month or two, a person in one of the vehicles is someone you know. Instead of nameless strangers, the victims are people you have talked to, worked with or engaged with in some way.

For the combat veteran, this type of event is ongoing. There is no way to predict when one of these events is going to occur, who is going to be involved or what the ultimate damage or outcome will be.

There is no other route for the combat veteran other than going AWOL. Going AWOL in a combat zone is desertion. It is subject to the most severe punishments the military can muster and brands the guilty as a coward for the rest of their lives.

No matter how many times the combat veteran sees a dead enemy, it still makes an impression. However, no matter how many times the combatant sees a dead comrade it makes an indention in their spirit that never really goes away.

Different thoughts can go through the soldier's mind when seeing a casualty. "Did he feel any pain?" is one of the most common thoughts. It springs from the idea that hopefully, if the fate befalls me I will not feel anything. However, the grotesque facial expressions and frozen body contortions often make it clear that the person's death was anything but quick and painless.

For the young warrior, the post-teenage soldier, seeing a dead comrade challenges their presupposed air of invincibility. "It could have been me," runs through their mind and brings an unwelcomed awareness of their vulnerability.

A thought that Christian believers have is, "But for the grace of God there go I." It is a reminder to the combatant that God is still in charge and, for some reason, they have been spared. "Man, what a shame," was a common reaction for us as was, "He deserved better."

From what I have learned, these are the healthier types of thoughts we should have, and during my first few months in Nam that is how I reacted. It is healthy for humans to have compassion for other humans who have experienced a significant trauma. That is part of what "love your enemy" is all about, I think. People are people and when we lose our sensitivity to the suffering of others we begin to lose our own humanity.

By the time I left Vietnam, my reaction to seeing a dead enemy soldier was, "Good," or "Good riddance."

What had happened to shift my thinking, and the thinking of too many combat veterans, to such an uncaring level?

First Kill "Can I do it?"

If a pre-combat soldier is not asking that question of himself he is not seriously considering his future. Squeezing the trigger of a gun pointed at another human being and knowing that the outcome could mean certain death for the other person is not something anyone should take lightly.

For me the test came our second month on Hill 55 between fingers three and four. We had set up there because of suspected activity in the wire during the previous nights. If a gook was trying to sneak in, they were doing so in a way not to trip the flares or the mines we had in the wire.

Some tin cans with a few rocks inside of them were tied to the wire. The idea was that any movement in the wire would cause a rattling noise even if the flares and mines were not tripped. Sometimes the low tech approach is the best, especially when the enemy knows how to avoid the more sophisticated obstacles.

Sure enough, about two in the morning, we heard the rattle. Our natural night vision had kicked in meaning our pupils were as dilated as they could be and we could see fairly well in the semidarkness.

The jeep was running and the engine noise did nothing to scare away the person in the wire. I rotated the control knob to infrared, wide beam and saw the person in the wire. I rotated the knob to narrow beam and had the person illuminated like an actor on a stage.

It was eerie. There was a tiny figure wearing the familiar pointed straw hat and appearing to be dressed in black pajamas. Slowly and carefully working their way through the wire, they had made themselves an easy target.

Since alerting the others might give the intruder a reason to run, I reached for my M16, wrapped my hand around the pistol grip on the rifle, released the safety and raised the weapon to my shoulder with my right hand. With my left hand I changed the beam from infrared to white, illuminating the intruder.

I sighted in on the torso, the largest target on the human body, as I had been taught, squeezed off a round and the body slumped immediately. Others fired rounds in the same direction I had fired and then we waited. Had I hit the target, had someone else or was the intruder playing possum?

No noise, no movement, it must have been a single individual.

The body was clearly distinguishable. A sweep of the area did not show evidence of any other enemy activity so a squad of grunts was called in to retrieve the body. Since there were mines in the wire and we did not know exactly where they were, the decision was made to wait until dawn. .

At sunup I walked with the patrol as they went out to where the body was draped over the concertina. The squad leader walked the wire for about one hundred feet in each direction, saw no mines and set out to retrieve the enemy's carcass. The concertina was cut in a couple of places to make it easier to get in and drag out the body from the perimeter defense.

As soon as the body was moved and flipped over, we saw it. This was not a traditional Viet Cong; it was an old woman, probably someone's grandmother.

I had my first kill. I had proven to myself that I could pull the trigger. But the first kill was a grandmother. Would I be able to pull the trigger the next time?

I went numb. I turned away just in time to vomit up the C-Rations from the night before. For the next two days I could not eat – I was <u>being</u> eaten by what was going on inside of me.

Of course this was not the type of thing most of us wrote home about. For me, this was probably the defining moment that was the beginning of the chasm that would separate the two Chucks.

The second day after the event I attended the daily briefing at the command bunker. The kill had been mentioned the day before, the day of the incident, but little was known. By this time the local Vietnamese liaison had investigated and the following details were added to the record. It was indeed an old woman. She had two grenades on her body and had apparently dropped one when she was shot – it was found a few feet from the body. The body was returned to the small village at the bottom of the hill and the village chief said that she was crazy and had exhibited bizarre behavior in the past.

So I had shot a crazy old woman who was attempting to bring grenades close enough to throw them at us? All I could think about was I had shot a woman.

Slowly the appetite returned. Between the troop ship diet and the first kill diet I thought it best not to send home any pictures of myself. I was beginning to hide the new Chuck. The chasm between the old me and the emerging me would now impact the relationship with my family.

The flashbacks of this incident have been shrouded in dark clouds. Recently I realized the image always appeared green, indicating I had seen her with the infrared even though my recollection had been different. I wake up at night and feel the crosshatch of the pistol grip on the M16 digging into the fingers and palm on my right hand. I sometimes hear the sound of the M16 round being fired – an unmistakable, explosion that signals a bullet has been launched that cannot be retrieved.

While I would fire my M16 many more times in Nam, I preferred the grenade launcher or calling in mortars and artillery because they were less personal. They were less intimate.

A STEADY DIET CHANGES BEHAVIOR

The human mind and the human body are remarkable machines. They can adapt to the unexpected in ways we cannot imagine. As the psalmist, David, said, "We are fearfully and wonderfully made."

Our young bodies were going into survival mode by adapting to the tropical heat and humidity while also learning to function on the strange diet of C-Rations. C-Rations can create constipation – a welcomed malady in a combat zone where latrines are hard to find. However, our monthly malaria tablet had just the opposite effect and created a queue line at the latrine.

Our minds were going into survival mode as well. This was not necessarily a good thing. Just as we learned to ignore the tropical climate, the taste of C-Rations and the other physical discomforts, we were training our minds to ignore the things our sight, hearing and sense of smell were experiencing.

If we had continued to internalize and think about the carnage we were experiencing it would have been more difficult to maintain our sanity.

We came up with terms that made discussing those things easier. When a person was killed we would say they "bought the farm". If they were shot and wounded, they were "dinged". If they were burned to death, the most horrible imaginable death, they were "crispy crittered".

It was important for us to desensitize ourselves from the inevitabilities of war. I imagine most combat veterans in all wars have done the same.

## MORE THAN DYING

The United States military trains their warriors to wound rather than to kill their adversaries. The thinking is that if an enemy soldier is wounded on the battlefield another soldier will come along and help rescue him. So wounding one warrior can remove two or three from the battle as comrades attempt to remove their wounded from harm's way.

That thinking assumes that the enemy has the same respect for human life as we do. The wars in Iraq and Afghanistan have demonstrated that some combatants allow their hatred of the enemy to override their compassion for their comrades. They will ignore the needs of a fellow warrior to have another shot at the enemy. Our Western tendency is to save our comrade before continuing the battle.

In Iraq and Afghanistan the enemy used Improvised Explosive Devices, IEDs. These are built using whatever explosives the enemy can find and are detonated by trip wires, cell phones and other triggers.

The Viet Cong took killing to the next level. Their goal was to kill as many enemy combatants as possible and at the same time disable or demoralize as many others as they could. They had limited access to exploding devices, so most of their improvised devices were crude – and effective: they would kill or grotesquely mutilate a warrior and in doing so they would demoralize at the same time.

Their most effective tool for accomplishing this was the use of vicious, cruel killing devices. Most were made of bamboo. Bamboo was plentiful in South Vietnam, grows quickly and is a familiar material for the Vietnamese.

It is a highly versatile material. It can be shaped into a knife that will cut as well as a steel knife. It can be shaped into a barbed spearhead that embeds itself into a human body and does more damage being removed than it did when it entered. The VC learned that they could put disgusting substances, like urine, poison, etc., on the points and make the wound even more destructive.

These bamboo spears would be placed in the bottom of a pit, known as a punji pit, pointed upwards and then have the pit camouflaged so that the enemy would fall into it and be impaled on the spears. Only one or two soldiers or Marines would fall into the pit but the others who witnessed it would be traumatized by the sight, sound and smell.

Watching their fellow Marine walking one minute and then writhing in unimaginable pain with bamboo spears protruding from their bodies would seriously demoralize the other troops.

Another use of bamboo would be to have a number of these spears embedded in a bamboo stalk. Then they would bend back the stalk and hold it with a trip wire. When an unsuspecting American warrior tripped the wire, the stalk would slap his body and embed the spears from head to toe.

There were as many variations on these uses as there were VC.

Word of these traps would spread. The military leaders were trying to educate the ground warriors on what to look for when out in the field. So the instructors would describe in detail how the booby traps were designed, how they worked and the grotesque results they produced. Their goal was to inform and motivate the soldiers in the field.

The result, however, was a demoralization of the troops.

Squads of grunts were sent out at night to look for enemy activity. These were called listening posts or LPs or Lurps. The six or eight men would go out to a specific set of coordinates on the map and set up a perimeter which was essentially every man facing in a different direction in a circle. Whatever direction the enemy moved around, one of the members of the squad would see them. There could be no verbal communication because Charlie would hear it. So hand signals were used for the troops in the field and keying the microphone on the radio would be used to communicate with those of us on the hill.

As they walked from the hill to their intended spot, the radio-man would call in check points: CP or "Charlie Papa". The first check point was usually the near side of the bridge; the second would be the other side of the bridge, etc. The purpose of the check points was to know where the squad was. If we lost contact with them we knew they would be somewhere between two checkpoints.

These LPs were expected to go out after dark so Charlie figured out he could set a booby trap at dusk and the LP, unable to detect it, would walk into it after dark.

The LPs headed towards the south side of the hill would usually come out to finger five with us to allow their eyes to adjust to the dark. Natural night vision is a learned skill and relies on the eyes being shielded from light for a period of time. So the Lurps would sit with us for a while before heading down to the bridge.

As the reports of booby traps in our area increased, the LPs began spending the entire night on finger five. Instead of going out and risking an encounter with a booby trap, they would risk punishment by staying with us.

After dark, we would be sitting around talking softly and watching the jungle below. At certain times the radioman would raise his hand and we would all be quiet as he radioed in, "Charlie Papa one", and the command center would think they were approaching the near side of the bridge. A few minutes later he would repeat the process, "Charlie Papa two" and the command center would think they were on the far end of bridge.

Just before the sun came up, the Lurps were supposed to make their way to our side of the bridge. Then, at first light, I would hear the radio operator sitting beside me speak into his microphone, "Charlie Papa seven" followed by "Charlie Papa six". They were "making their way back to the hill".

When the sun finally came up, the LP would be at the end of the bridge ready to come back up on the hill if anyone should be watching.

CRUELTY BACKFIRES

After we had experienced enough of the Viet Cong's cruelty, it began to work against them. We lost any semblance of civility in our firefights. We had long abandoned the rules of the Geneva Convention and were now breaking our own rules.

Originally we would not intentionally shoot livestock, like water buffalo for instance. The peasants in our area depended on these huge beasts to plow their rice paddies and perform other tasks. Tiny Vietnamese boys would use sticks to beat these animals into submission so they weren't as fierce as they appeared.

The VC would go into a local's hooch and shoot at us knowing we would not return the fire for fear of hitting the civilians who lived there. Once their cruelty became more intense, the VC were fair game no matter where they were. Besides, we figured, the locals knew where the booby traps had been placed and failed to tell us for fear that the VC would punish them – which they would, of course.

The civilians were in a no-win situation. If they helped us during the day, the VC would punish them at night. If they helped the VC we probably would not know it so it is easy to understand where their allegiance would be. All they wanted to do was to get up in the morning and grow rice. They would understandably do whatever was necessary to survive.

One night we were taking incoming small arms fire from a hooch we had been protecting. The old mama-san and papa-san who lived there were simply caught in a bad spot. During the day they liked us; at night they liked the VC. It was simply a matter of survival. The fire was coming from a pen outside the hooch, so I used the infrared to try and find Charlie.

Through the infrared binoculars all I could see was the reflection of two eyes. Human eyes do not reflect light; the eyes of many animals do. I knew I was seeing their precious water buffalo and I also knew Charlie was there somewhere.

The tank had moved to my left in response to the incoming fire and the TC was looking at me. I pointed to the 90 MM and then pointed to the hooch. He understood. When he gave me a thumbs-up signal indicating the round was loaded and ready to fire, I changed the light beam from infrared to white so the tank's gunner could see the target. He moved the turret slightly, moved the barrel down a few degrees and a 90 MM explosive round destroyed the pen, the water buffalo and the hooch. Hopefully it took out the VC as well.

For all we knew the mama-san and papa-san who lived there had become "collateral" damage. They hadn't, as it turned out. There had been a time when that mattered.

The next morning the papa-san and another man brought the head of the water buffalo up to the command center and were given a relatively large amount of money to replace the animal. The Marines who were on watch that day saw him and the other man take the head to another hill a mile away and collect another payment. They left that outpost and headed to another, probably to collect again, but disappeared in the jungle. Losing a water buffalo could be a profitable endeavor that resulted in replacing it with a younger, stronger one and still having some money left over.

For all we knew, the other man carrying the severed head was a Viet Cong.

As we lost respect for the enemy we also lost respect for the locals. We were already losing respect for the military and their rules. Without realizing it, we were losing respect for ourselves.

We wanted other Americans to engage in cruel ways of killing so that what we were doing wouldn't seem so bad. So there were massacres and in those massacres civilians were killed and some of those civilians were babies. Perhaps the term "baby killers" had a particular sting because we knew that on very rare occasions some of us may have inadvertently been guilty of that atrocity.

Military maps show different types of structures such as churches, hospitals and schools. According to the Geneva Convention, these places are off limits. The enemy used them just as they do today in the Middle East wars. Positioning themselves and their weapons around civilians and protected buildings is a way of keeping civilized people from firing on them.

Most combat veterans see the use of schools, churches and homes for firing positions as the activity of a coward.

I had respect for the Buddhist religion even though I knew little about it. The religion requires their believers to have shrines in their homes. More affluent – or perhaps more "religious" – Buddhists would have larger shrines known as pagodas. The only time we used the word pagoda was in reference to these shrines. Some were very ornate and had been around for generations. They were off limits and the gooks knew it.

A few days after some body bags passed through the hill on their way back to the rear, we were hit by a contingent of what seemed to be local Viet Cong. On the truck with the body bags there were three or four body bags containing dead Americans as well as eight or ten Vietnamese in civilian clothes stacked randomly around the bags on the truck. With the body bags fresh on our minds we engaged the enemy. One VC was crouched behind a large, ornate pagoda in the middle of a rice paddy firing at us with an AK-47. I had the focused beam of the searchlight trained on the pagoda so that when he stuck his head out to fire someone could see him.

We were intentionally avoiding any direct hits on the pagoda when I heard the whine of the turret on the tank. I looked up just in time to hear the simultaneous boom and the ping of the 90MM being fired and then turned my head to see the pagoda disintegrate and a body cartwheel in the air.

We would be less popular with the locals as a result of this firefight but we were beyond the point of caring.

A steady diet of killing was no longer interrupting our other appetites.

### P.T.S.D.

*The combat warrior sees their share of mutilated and dead bodies. Each makes an impression. The ones that will not go away are the ones that the warrior created. Initially unbearable, the trauma that accompanies these actions has to be suppressed or the warrior will become his own worst enemy; any reluctance to pull the trigger could be fatal. The worst possible trauma, it would seem, would be the warrior who kills some of his own comrades. Referred to by the misnomer of "friendly fire", it is a form of PTSD that is virtually impossible to cure.*

*For me, killing an armed enemy soldier would become easier – not easy at first, just easier as events unfolded. Killing an unarmed woman was way over the top*

# CHAPTER NINE
## Summertime and the Living Is Easy

Hill 55: Months Three and Four 210 Days To Go

S pring turned into summer on Hill 55 but the only indication of the transition was the calendar. The weather was not appreciably different.

Charlie seemed to be taking some time off. We would go days without a party and some of the parties were short; mostly Lurps spotting some activity and the rest of us assisting.

A Marine fighter jet screamed overhead from the DaNang airbase every night followed by another just like it, only upside down. It was his way of signaling his brother, it turns out, a platoon commander on the hill. Hill 55 was the right distance from the airbase for the jets to kick in their afterburners right overhead. It was an impressive sight and sound.

One night the first jet came screaming at us, kicked on the afterburner and went dark and silent. The plane fell like a brick and the pilot ejected. There was only one parachute so we never learned the fate of the second crewman on the plane. We sent a squad out to find him and stayed up all night trying. Later that morning, before noon, the pilot made his way on his own to the road and flagged down a Marine vehicle.

For Station Break 44 it was the best of times.

Our situation was improving regularly. We had found an old, old wing tank which had held fuel on some airplane while the French had been in Vietnam. Someone had already modified the tank for use as a shower and had welded a plate and a half-inch pipe on the bottom. We decided to make a shower for ourselves so we assembled some lumber and hoisted the tank up on the frame.

We needed a valve to go on the pipe sticking out of the bottom of the tank and, remarkably, the Marine supply sergeant had one. It was old, bent and rusty, but it worked and was spring loaded. All we had to do was attach it on the pipe, put a piece of rope on it and then whenever we pulled the rope water would flow out of the pipe.

We began scrounging jerry cans, the five gallon cans the military uses for all things liquid. When the lids were missing or the cans were severely damaged or rusted, they would be set aside. We needed them to fill the shower tank. Once we had collected a trailer full of jerry cans, we started making runs down to the river to fill them. There was a gasoline powered pump on the river bank so filling the cans was not much of a chore. When the jeep and trailer returned to the shower, the water cans had to be lifted up and emptied into the wing tank. That was a chore.

We had fashioned a ladder and so we made a bucket brigade and passed the cans up one at a time until all were emptied. Now we had a shower.

Davis inaugurated it. With his towel over his shoulder, he walked under the tank, stripped buck naked and pulled the rope. Then he screamed.

We had not factored in water temperature.

Over time we got used to the cold water and, besides, we did not take showers all that often. The Marines asked to use the shower so we made a deal that anyone using it had to help fill it and it became the community shower.

## A Fortuitous Trip to the Rear

On one of our trips to the rear I went down to the supply tent for something. To prove that miracles, or perhaps incompetence, still exist, Whittaker was in charge of the supply tent. The Army had put the fox in charge of the hen house.

The supply sergeant had gone somewhere and someone had put the good Sergeant Whittaker in charge. He and I got along fine which was an uncommon occurrence for him since most people tried to avoid him.

Finally I told him what I needed and he retrieved it. Then he began giving me things I had not requested or even knew existed. He would go back and return with an armload of things and ask, "You guys have any of these?" Of course we didn't so he saw to it that we did.

While we were chatting I mentioned our shower and Whittaker held up a finger, disappeared and returned with a plastic shower head!

Maybe it was because he enjoyed scrounging or being around other scroungers but whatever it was, he pulled off the ultimate coup. "Your guys are entitled to a hooch, did you know that?" "Yeah, they came out and set it up. It's actually only half a hooch. One of my guys and I sleep in it and we all cook in it and when it rains we all huddle in it."

Whittaker looked at me and laughed. "In the field you're entitled to an entire hooch even if you only have four guys."

"We have five, "I said.

"Whatever," Whittaker replied, "we'll send the other half out tomorrow." And they did.

Now we had a bunker that would sleep three, a hooch that would sleep the other two and an additional hooch that would be our living quarters, our own day room.

Life was getting better.

A chaplain was showing up two or three times a month and holding non-denominational services and I found them comforting even though the message was close to meaningless. How does a chaplain say anything that will appeal to Protestants, Catholics and Jews without being offensive? Essentially the message was "God is good, do good."

RATS

There was the ongoing issue with the rats, however.

On a mail run, the folks in the rear brought us some mouse traps, the types you see in the grocery store. We did not have mice; we had rats. Big rats. These critters were the size of house cats and mouse traps weren't going to do any good. (Although the cheese they sent along as bait was pretty tasty.)

We had requested rat traps, not mouse traps.

The Marines came to the rescue. They had rat traps. Their traps were made of chicken wire, were about the size of a shoebox and had a trap door on one end. A rat would walk into the chicken wire box, go to the far end for the bait and the door would close behind them. It trapped the rat but it did not kill it.

Most of the rats we caught this way would work their feet out the bottom and walk around the bunker wearing the cage like a costume. When we returned to the bunker and the trap was not where it was supposed to be, we knew there was a trap-wearing rat walking around somewhere.

Then we had to decide what to do with the rat.

Martin did not hesitate. He simply picked up the trap and his M16, went outside and shot the rat. As good as that idea might sound, and certainly seemed to be a good one to Martin at the time, it is not the best way. Shooting a small animal at close range with a high powered rifle whose projectile is designed to tumble on impact results in the small animal virtually exploding. We had rat pieces everywhere.

The next rat was taken a distance away from the bunker and every other structure and shot there.

I came back to the bunker from a daily briefing and found everyone outside the bunker standing in a circle. Another rat had been caught and would be disposed of in a whole new way. Several Marines had joined us and would witness the execution.

Martin had dug a circular trench about four feet in diameter and filled it with diesel fuel. Holding the rat by the tail, he dipped the animal in diesel fuel, had Smith light the diesel in the trench and then, when the trench was a flaming halo, Martin threw the rat in the middle.

Naturally, the rat ran away. In so doing, he ran through the flames, caught on fire and continued running into a ditch where he flopped around and died.

The Marines cheered. This was the best entertainment Hill 55 had ever had.

Word spread quickly. A couple of hours later we were loading the jeeps to go out for the night and the Marines yelled to us that they had caught a rat and were about to do an encore performance.

Since we were loaded and on our way out, we drove the jeeps down to their communications bunker where the night's entertainment would be.

The circular trench was ready and full of diesel. Someone dipped the rat in diesel fuel, someone else lit the trench and the rat was thrown in the circle. Just as before, the rat made a run for it, became rodent flambé, but decided to run into the communications bunker.

This was an unexpected and unfortunate event. The smell of burning rat is almost as bad as the smell of burned rat.

The Marines chased the critter into the bunker and were using a broom and rifle butts in an attempt to sweep him out. We headed out to our assignments for the night.

The next morning we returned and headed for the bunker when we saw all of the radios lined up outside the communications bunker. A lone radio operator sat out in the open on an ammo box with headphones on his head. I couldn't tell if he was awake or asleep but he didn't wave at us.

The communications bunker would not be occupied for a few more days.

SHARING THE POWER

One day one of the grunts who lived in the communications bunker came by and asked about our electric fan. Now that ventilation was more important for them they were considering having an electric fan. He wanted to know where we were getting our electricity.

I did not want to admit to anything so I asked, "Where is there electricity on the hill?"

"Well, the command bunker has electricity but it's too far away and I'm not going to fool with the Major's stuff."

"Where else?" I asked and I turned and looked to the east where finger two where Hawk missile unit was.

"Oh, the Hawk Missile guys!" We could not see the missiles because of the ridge line. "They have two big generators."

"Yes, one is a sixty-cycle generator and the other is the four-hundred cycle for their radar. Do you know the difference?"

"Not really"

I explained as well as I could. "The sixty-cycle generator is what we're used to. The four-hundred cycle might work okay for light bulbs but it will burn out any motor that plugs into it."

The Marine thought for a minute and asked, "How do we tell the difference?"

"Well," I started, "the current rating will be on the designation plate but it may be hard to find and read – especially at night." I assumed they would be tapping into the generator at night as we had done. "The easiest way to tell is the one on the right is the sixty-cycle."

Unfortunately I had not given specific instructions about right and left. I meant right from where we were standing and he assumed it would be the one on the right for the missile battery. That would be the opposite.

Then the Marine asked for help in knowing how to connect the wires. "Okay, as you approach the generator you will see one side has wires attached to a metal box near the ground. Open the lid to the box and you will see two metal bars with screws on them. Attach one of your wires to one bar and the other to the other bar. Make sure you close the lid so no one will know you've been there."

"Got it," he said.

It was several days later when the Marine returned and asked me to check out the wiring in his bunker. "A couple of guys hooked it up last night and we're ready to check it out," he said. "But if we wired it wrong it could blow a fuse and the missile people will find out what we've done."

"Did you hook up to the right generator?" I asked.

"I wasn't there but I gave them the instructions you gave me."

Davis and I accompanied him down to their bunker and were greeted by a whiff of fried rat when we walked in.

The wiring in the bunker would be pretty straight forward and difficult to screw up. We walked through it all beginning where their buried wires came in through some sandbags and continued through a few light bulb sockets and a couple of outlets.

The last outlet was below a ventilation slot and already had a brand new electric fan plugged in. "Looks good to me, "I said.

And with that the Marine turned on the fan.

The brand new fan immediately revved up and then with a scream and flying sparks pushed itself backwards towards us. It took on a life of its own. It proceeded to die almost as quickly as it had started. A pitiful trail of smoke came out of the carcass of the fan that had been pushed to run at seven times its intended speed.

We stood around silent and motionless staring at the smoking remains.

Finally, the Marine spoke. "Wrong generator."

ANOTHER IMPROVEMENT

One other improvement we made to our situation was changing the shower water from cold to not as cold. The goal was to have hot water but we could not figure that one out. Back in the rear the showers had emersion heaters in them that heated the water. These were essentially diesel burners that were designed to be submerged in water with a chimney rising above the water level.

Try as we did, we could not procure an emersion heater. Instead, Davis came up with the idea of partially submerging a five gallon bucket in the wing tank with the top of the bucket above the water level. We added rocks to the bucket, poured in diesel fuel, lit it and let the hot rocks warm the water.

It kind of worked. The water around the bucket warmed up slightly so that the first person to take a shower had a few minutes of not-so-cold water.

Our goal was clear: we had to find an emersion heater. It would take months, as it turned out, but ultimately we would succeed.

## A Quieter Finger Five

Nights on finger five were settling down. There were few parties and we enjoyed long conversations with the tank crew.

One night someone brought a copy of the military newspaper, "The Stars and Stripes" and we read about the Six Day War in the Middle East. The Israelis had kicked some serious butt in a very short time. We looked at the pictures of the burned-out tanks, the convoys that had been completely annihilated and saw that more damage had been done in that war that we had seen in months of combat in Nam.

Since the nights were quieter, I began sleeping on the hood of the jeep curled up in a ball. Young bodies can do that. Whenever Martin sensed something was going on, he would start the jeep and by the time he slid down to the gun, I would be on the light. He would point in the general direction and I would scan the area with either the white light or the infrared.

This extra sleep would make it easier for me to function during the day while the others slept.

## Daily Briefings

Each day I would go up to the command bunker at 4 PM for the daily briefing. A representative from each unit on the hill would attend and be informed about enemy activity in the area as well as what activities the Americans would be engaging in during the night. The 105 MM artillery battery was usually represented by the mission control officer, a first lieutenant. The 80 MM mortar group had no officers so an E-5 usually showed up for them. The tank battery commander, a captain, came for most briefings.

The senior officer for the grunts, which changed from captain to lieutenant and back to captain again several times, was always the most strategic person. After all, he represented the men who would be moving around in the jungle at the bottom of the hill, manning the bridge and accompanying us on the various fingers. The Hawk Missile commander, a captain, attended every briefing but there were never indications of Viet Cong aircraft that would require his attention.

The 80 MM mortar guy and I were the only NCOs in these briefings; everyone else was an officer.

Friendly fire was a real problem so knowing where the friendlies *were* and *were not* supposed to be was important.

I would carry my acetate-covered map with me and use a grease pencil to mark areas of interest.

One night on my way to the briefing I saw two German shepherds and their handlers standing outside the bunker. The dogs were separated and each was leashed to a sturdy post. The two handlers were talking. I introduced myself and joined their conversation to learn how the dogs were deployed.

Some new tunnels had been found nearby and these dogs were to be used to find them. I learned about the dogs as they talked. First of all, a dog could only have one handler. Any other person, even another handler, would be attacked by the dog since its first allegiance was to protect its handler. I learned that it took more time and cost more money to bring a dog up to speed than it did a soldier or Marine. So, when faced with the choice of evacuating an injured dog or an injured handler, the dog was to go first.

The dogs had to be kept separated because if either dog came close to the other's handler that would be seen as a threat and it was almost impossible to break them apart once they began fighting.

While we were talking, the dogs stared at us and at each other. One of them was mostly black; the other mostly brown and was known as Queenie. The name did not fit. From reports, this was the most vicious German Shepherd in Vietnam. Both handlers agreed on this point.

If there was such a thing as a psychotic dog, Queenie was it. "She hates gooks," Queenie's handler said. "Once she latches on to one, she will not let go."

As we continued to talk, both dogs turned and began facing the road. Immediately they were up on all fours and growling. "Gook," Queenie's handler said.

Sure enough, in a moment the South Vietnamese Army, ARVN, liaison officer appeared. This was the guy who was responsible for coordinating our activities with the ARVN's and for interacting with the Vietnamese locals. What he did best was keep his starched and polished uniform spotless. For all we knew he could have worked for the enemy; one thing we did know was that he was all out for himself. As a result, he was not invited to the daily briefings even though that would have seemed to be a logical use of his abilities.

Once the liaison officer saw the dogs, he froze. One of the handlers waved him up and he began walking again.

As he approached Queenie, she sat down and began whimpering and waging her tail. She appeared to be as approachable as any domestic puppy. What a sweet doggie!

The liaison officer began walking towards her with his hand out to pat her on the head when the handler stopped him. With an unmistakably stern voice he told the officer to move along.

Turning back to me he said, "That's her favorite trick. She acts docile and then, when the person reaches out their hand to pat her, she latches on to their arm!" He laughed. "I can't get her to turn loose."

Turning to the dog he commanded, "Queenie, DOWN!" The dog laid down seemingly disappointed with the events of the past few minutes.

In Vietnam, even the animals became more evil.

## P.T.S.D.

*Recreation now involved torturing animals and laughing about it. I had sunk to a new low. We spent our days "out of uniform" since wearing shirts, even jungle shirts when we could get them, would cause us to overheat. The smells of diesel, an open latrine and the body odors from many warriors crammed into a small area were now accepted parts of our environment. Stealing - food from the rear and electricity from other units - was acceptable behavior. Morals were being abandoned and would need to be reestablished when we got back home.*

# CHAPTER TEN
## Operation Arizona

Hill 55 Month Five 150 Days to Go

**M**ONSOON SEASON

We had been warned about the rain but being from the South where rainstorms are legendary, I didn't take the warnings that seriously.

It began raining and it never stopped. We got wet and never seemed to get dry.

A letter home prompted my father to send me a rain suit from Sears. It was olive green, kept me mostly dry and was comfortable even in a firefight. It was not military-issue nor did it meet any of the military's requirements. But it was dry.

Then the typhoon hit. We were used to the rain, the constant mud in our living quarters and caked on the jeeps. We were not expecting the wind that accompanied the typhoon that was several miles offshore.

Martin and I huddled in the jeep all night long, shivering at times. In retrospect, we should not have gone out to finger five that night. The few times we turned on the light it mirrored off the thick sheets of rain and only managed to illuminate us. We literally could not see three feet from our face. We had my poncho covering one side of the jeep and a tarp covering the other side. Still, too much water got through.

The tank crew was buttoned up. Occasionally they would start their engine to warm and ventilate the tank but they were stuck just as we were. I felt sorry for the grunts. I had no idea where they were or how they were surviving the deluge.

There was some radio chatter, mostly from the bridge. They had to scramble to stay above the rising river.

We were as vulnerable as we would ever be. The enemy could have walked right up to us without being seen. We kept our rifles close and waited for the sun to come up so we could go back to the bunker.

That turned out to be wishful thinking.

The sunlight revealed an unpleasant surprise. Finger five was now an island. The river had risen, the valley floor was flooded and there was no escape from the finger until the water receded.

Another problem was the snakes. Some snakes don't like water so they seek higher ground and higher ground at this time was finger five. There was a green snake that was referred to as a "two-stepper". If it bit someone, they could take about two steps before the snake's venom did its work.

There were green snakes all over the finger and we learned how difficult it is to shoot one with a bullet.

Fortunately, the Marines are the amphibious assault unit for the Navy which means they have the ability to move around in water. They brought us some C Rats and by the afternoon the water level was low enough for the jeep to ford its way back to the hill.

The grunts and tank had stayed with us even though they could have returned earlier. That's the way it is with the Marines. They leave no one behind. No one.

Monsoon season ended and it did not take long for the hot tropical sun to dry out everything and go back to baking anything under it.

OPERATION ARIZONA

For the most part the Marines left us alone in the mornings while we slept so it was an unusual occurrence for me to be awakened by a Marine corporal around ten. "Major Huffman wants you at the command bunker on the double."

Major Huffman was a seasoned Marine officer right out of central casting. In his late forties, he had the same three-inch stub of a cigar in his mouth the entire time I knew him. He barked orders and was genuinely concerned about all aspects of the morale and condition of his men. As the senior officer on Hill 55 he was ultimately responsible for everything that went on there.

He was as tough as he was fair. The major ran a tight ship and maintained order on the hill while earning the respect of more men than usual. There is always grumbling in the ranks but with Major Huffman almost everyone agreed he was the type of leader we needed. He was respected by everyone I knew but there were probably some who did not like him – there always are.

He ran our daily briefings and gave us the intelligence, the G2, on what was going on in our area. About the only interaction he and I had was when he barked his orders for where we would set up the lights each night. "Eveready," he would say, "you'll be on finger five and finger one." I would nod or say, "Yes, sir!" and that would end our conversation. I could figure out the details.

The Old Man had been out to talk with him a few times checking up on our performance. His goal was to find reasons for punishing us. The major always backed us up and told the captain what a valuable resource we were for them.

The major was the consummate officer who would never undermine the authority of another officer. All he ever said to me about the Old Man's visits were during the briefings and then all he would say was, "Eveready, your battery commander was out today." Then he would give me our assignments for the night. As I left one briefing, the major's orderly and I were walking out of the command bunker together and he told me the major referred to the Old Man as the "Little Prick".

It would have been foolish to take for granted the relationship we had with the major. He did not tolerate familiarity or any sign of weakness. So when the order came to report to the command bunker, I went as quickly as I could. Rather than walk up, I took one of the jeeps and drove up.

When I entered the familiar bunker, a Marine NCO with an M14 on his shoulder asked me for my ID. That had never happened before on my daily visits. Satisfied with what he saw, he handed back the card and pointed to a doorway that led into a section of the bunker I had not seen before. When I entered the small room, I saw the major in an adjacent room sitting in a chair and looking at a large map spread out on a field table.

"Come in, Eveready," the major said and motioned me in.

We did not salute in Vietnam, even indoors. Still, my respect for the man at the table was as high as for anyone I had known.

A single light bulb hung from a wire overhead and the bulb could not have been more than forty watts. It wasn't bright but it was enough.

There were colored lines drawn on the map in various places and those seemed to be the focus of the major's attention. "Operation Arizona, Eveready, begins tonight." He put his finger on the map and I recognized it as Hill 55. "One of your lights is going out to support a frontal assault." As he began to speak, he traced his finger down the road to the bridge, across it, to the other side and then through a village and then deep into the jungle. His finger stopped at a river some twenty miles away.

"The report is that there is an NVA unit moving in from the other side of this river. It's huge. They may even have armor; we know they have mobility."

This was a game changer. We were supposed to be fighting weak little Vietnamese rag tag units. The NVA was a modern and relatively sophisticated army. This giant mass of men and materials was coming in through Laos and was bringing rockets and other powerful weapons. Even though the Ho Chi Minh Trail was being bombed continuously by the American B-52's, supplies were pouring into I Corps and points south.

We thought an all-out assault was eminent but we were wrong. This was all designed as a build up for the TET Offensive four months later. These were patient people and someone, somewhere was doing some sophisticated planning. In hindsight, this activity would explain some of the other new and different encounters we would have.

"There is still a lot of planning going on but here are your initial orders. You are to take one of your units to these coordinates. There you will be joined by an escort, probably a tank, maybe a Pig, and be escorted to the position where you are needed. There you will follow the direction of the senior in-command."

I wrote down the coordinates. My head was spinning. This was a different exercise than we had ever done and was a part of a war we had not fought before.

"Eveready, this is top secret. You cannot discuss it with anyone who does not have a need to know. Your commanding officer has been alerted but you cannot refer to this in any way in any communication. Is that clear?"

"Yes, sir." My mouth was working but my mind was in hyper-drive.

"Questions...?" The major finally looked up from the map.

"I will need a map of the area."

"There is one waiting for you with the orderly along with frequencies, authentication codes and call signs."

"How long will we be out?"

"Take enough rations for ten days. Resupply may be spotty."

I hesitated for a minute and then the major said, "If you have other questions, ask the orderly. Dismissed!"

He had more important things to do.

With that I left the major and his map and went to find the orderly. He went over the papers and the map and stressed several times how critical it was that no one know what I had just learned and how important it was to secure the papers and map. Any leaked information could end up causing American casualties.

There were multiple radio frequencies and below each one were the units that would be operating on those channels. I would need to determine who had the information I needed at any given time and then jump on their frequency to communicate. The position of the radio in the jeep, under the searchlight, made it impossible to change frequencies when we were driving. So, to contact anyone we would need to stop the jeep, I would get out and get on my knees wher I could read the radio controls and change the frequency. This would be interesting.

I went outside and sat in the jeep trying to collect my thoughts. Who would go out on the Operation? I would be one, I concluded, and Davis would be the other. Martin would be needed to manage the others in my absence.

A week in the woods was not attractive. We would lack the luxury of a rat-infested bunker, latrine or burner to heat C-Rations. Water would be a problem.

I drove the jeep down to the fuel truck and filled the gas tank and the five gallon can strapped on the back. This would be the jeep we took out on the op. We would also need to strap a full five gallon water can on the back of the jeep as well.

Then I decided I would start out with clean fatigues. A week without a bath would end better if my clothes were clean at the beginning of the odyssey.

Just inside the wire on finger two where the road came up on the hill there were some Vietnamese locals who did our laundry and offered haircuts. The proprietor was Jenny, a young Vietnamese woman who was looking for a husband and a trip to the United States.

Jenny had the best command of the English language of any of the workers and all of us had been asked many times, "You nice man – you take me to America?"

She was persistent.

Haircuts were given by old men using manual clippers. They knew one hairstyle and it closely resembled the first military haircuts we had received in basic training.

Clean laundry was set up in piles with our shirts folded neatly on top. This way we would know which pile was ours since our name tags would be showing.

I parked the jeep and hid the papers and map in a pouch behind the driver's seat. I could not risk these locals knowing anything about this massive, secret undertaking.

I walked down to their combination tent and shanty, found Jenny and told her I needed to pick up my laundry.

She gave me a big smile and said, "Okay! You go Operation Arizona?"

So much for the secrecy surrounding the planning of Operation Arizona; if Jenny knew, everyone knew.

If we were fooling anyone it was ourselves.

I drove the jeep back to the bunker and was surprised to see a three-quarter-ton truck sitting there. It was one of ours from base camp.

Inside the bunker I found our platoon sergeant, SSG Johnson, and his driver engaged in a conversation with Davis. It turned out that when the orderly came and woke me up he had also awakened Davis and shortly afterwards Johnson and his driver had arrived.

Their assignment was to brief me on the dos and don'ts related to Operation Arizona. Had I decided who would go was the first question. I had but I had not had a chance to discuss it with Davis. "It makes sense for me to go and I think Davis should go with me." I looked at Davis for his reaction but, as usual, he didn't react. Nothing seemed to faze him.

Since Davis and I were the only two awake, it made for fast conversation between us and Johnson. The good sergeant began telling us the rules.

SSG Johnson was a lifer and like most lifers did not like the idea of being in Nam. He was tall and lanky and generally unsure of himself. He seemed to fear authority more than respect it so maybe the Army was a good place for him.

I do not recall him ever standing up for one of his men. When the Old Man would jump on us, he would pile on rather than try to defend us. He was not the type of guy to ever make waves or decisions.

He nervously began telling us what he had been told to tell us and his approach began making me nervous.

We were not to take anything with us that would reveal who we were except for our dog tags. He would confiscate our ID cards and return them to us after the Operation if we returned. We were not to take any money with us. "If you are captured by the enemy..." I think he rattled off the line about only giving our name rank and serial number but my mind froze on the idea of being captured. That had not occurred to me. Remember, I was twenty years old and the portion of our brains that process consequences is not fully developed at that age.

The VC usually did not capture, they killed. Sadistically and as cruelly as they could in the time allotted, they would eliminate American soldiers physically in a way that would discourage other American soldiers mentally. The NVA who we would be engaging would take prisoners and no one knew what would happen to those unfortunate warriors.

We were to only take essentials: weapons, ammo, food and water. The Marines, he assured us, would be able to supply most of what we needed since we were supporting their operations.

This is how little the sergeant understood. On Hill 55, a semi-permanent installation, the Marines could not supply us. How were they going to have what we needed when everyone was on the move?

As he was leaving he told me that he and his driver were on their way to Hill 45 because one of their units would also be going on the op. That was Lindsey's position. I figured Lindsey would go out as well and probably take Corporal Bentley with him.

The sergeant asked if I had all the information I needed. I did not think I did – or ever would. I told him what I had received in the briefing and he said that was all I needed to know and that was that. In the back of my mind, I thought that if I needed any more information about Operations Arizona I would just go ask Jenny.

Davis and I talked for a while and made our plans for loading up. We would each write a letter home but we could not mail them until after the Operation. According to SSG Johnson, we didn't want the enemy to intercept our mail and read about Operation Arizona, something we were not inclined to write about anyway.

When the others woke up we explained what was going on. Martin would attend the daily briefing and determine where his jeep and gunner would go; Davis and I would be gone for an undetermined period of time.

Davis and I began assembling the stuff we would take. For each of us to have three meals a day for ten days would have been sixty C-Rations. That's five cases. We would take the machine gun and two boxes of ammo; the Marines would probably be able to resupply us ammo for the M60. We would each take our clips of M16 ammo but the Marines were using the M14s so we packed a couple of boxes of extra rounds we could use to reload our clips.

Davis would not be as proficient with the machine gun as Martin was; but he had qualified "Expert" and that was good enough for me.

Our tropical sleeping bags rolled up into small bundles and could be stuffed in the jeep below the light. We were not looking forward to sleeping on the ground and the cots we had in the bunker, which initially seemed like torture devices, were beginning to look comfy. We would try to find room for them on the jeep.

The pile of stuff was adding up. It would have been fine if we could have pulled a trailer, but we couldn't; we had to be as mobile and agile as possible.

I went to try and find some acetate to cover my new map and protect it from the elements and Davis said he would load the jeep. I was not successful; he was. When I returned to the bunker he had neatly loaded everything on the jeep including our now-folded cots. I could not believe he had found a way to load it all, but he did.

We somewhat resembled the opening scene of "The Beverly Hillbillies" television show except for the grandmother sitting on the top in a rocker.

We both took showers without soap – the gooks could smell our soap from a distance – and put on fresh fatigues and clean socks. We ate an early dinner and then headed out. We had pretty much obeyed SSG Johnson's list except that we did have all of our money with us. The Vietnamese locals we were supposedly protecting from Communism did not do anything for us without being paid and we did not know what help we might need.

With Davis driving and me navigating, we headed down to the bridge, crossed it and were able to look back and see Hill 55 disappearing. We drove through some small villages and the people there generally ignored us. They were used to military vehicles passing through, kicking up unwanted dust and making too much noise. They merely tolerated our presence.

Occasionally a young male would look sternly at us even as the jeep passed close enough to him for me to reach out and slap him. These young men were either refusing to serve in the South Vietnamese Army or were Viet Cong. We were eye to eye with them and there was nothing we could do about it.

When we arrived at the initial coordinates about an hour later, the sun was going down and we saw a large contingency of trucks, infantry and a couple of tanks. I looked for Lindsey but he was not there.

A marine came over to the jeep with no rank insignia on his shirt. This meant he was an officer and had removed his bars so the enemy would not single him out.

We all looked the same: green uniforms, flack vests, steel pots on our heads. Up close we could see the indention on the collar of the Marine officer's rank. Meanwhile the NCOs, like us, wore bold stripes on our sleeves.

There were no introductions or small talk, this guy was all business.

"You are to follow 67," he said and pointed to a tank whose serial number painted on the back ended in 67. "Call sign Yellow Cat 67, channel 4, they will take you to a rendezvous about here," he pointed to a place on my map, "where you will join a squad; they will take it from there."

With that, he turned and walked away.

I looked up channel 4 on the list I had received at the briefing, set the radio to the correct frequency and put on the headset. I put one earpiece on one ear keeping the other ear open so I could hear what was going on around us just as I did on the hill. Davis was already moving the jeep in position behind the tank.

There was noise and some occasional chatter on the radio.

I keyed the mike, "Yellow Cat 67 this is Station Break 44, radio check, over."

"Is that you doggie?" Radio protocol was not necessary.

"Roger, we are behind you, ready when you are."

The tank commander stuck his head up out of the turret, looked back at us and spoke into his radio, "Looks like you'll be breathing some serious exhaust tonight. Ever worked with a tank before?"

"Every night," I replied, "a blade on Hill 55; the TC is Skully."

"We trained together at Quantico, know him well. Stand by. Out."

His helmeted head dropped into the tank and out of sight. We waited.

Eventually all twelve cylinders of the tank's engine came to life and the initial cloud of smoke came at us. The turret swiveled right and left, the tube went up and down a few times and then the radio crackled. "Yellow Cat 6 this is Yellow Cat 67, over." The tank commander was checking in with someone, a lower number usually indicated higher rank and he was using protocol. This was his signal to everyone on that channel to be careful – the brass was listening.

"Yellow Cat 67 this is Yellow Cat 6, over."

"6, this is 67, ready to roll, over."

"Roger. Wait. Out."

There would be a delay. It was already getting dark.

After a few minutes the radio came to life again. "Yellow Cat 67, this is Yellow Cat 6, proceed to your Delta Zulu, drop your cargo and return, over."

"Roger, out."

The Delta Zulu, drop zone, in this case was where we would rendezvous with the squad of grunts somewhere near the river Major Huffman had shown me on the map that morning. Davis and I were the cargo.

The tank buttoned up and when the driver goosed the throttle, the tank reared back on its haunches and began moving forward. Tanks make a lot of noise. Between the low-pitched roar of the engine and the high-pitched squeaks coming from the tracks, it could be heard for long distances. When moving around at night, every hatch was closed, buttoned up, to prevent grenades and other ugliness from being tossed inside. The driver used periscopes to see where he was going.

"Station Break 44, this is Yellow Cat 67, what's your pos?" The TC wanted to know our position – were we following him? There was no rear view mirror on a tank.

"On you tail, over."

"Roger."

At first the drive was on dirt roads and occasionally we passed through small villages. The hooches were mostly dark except for a random candle or cooking fire, and the smell of Vietnamese cuisine would help overcome the smell of the tank's exhaust.

We drove for miles with our rifles at the ready. The headlights were off and we depended on Davis's night vision to keep us on the road and behind the tank.

The tank began slowing so I thought we were nearing the drop zone. Instead, it veered off the road, down a slight embankment and then began plowing through some elephant grass. The tank had no problem knocking down the tall, thick grass but the jeep was struggling.

The tank's track laid down the grass but Davis could not put the jeep's tires in the flattened grass. The tank was too wide so he could only use one trail laid down by the tank's track for the jeep.

Davis wisely put the left wheels of the jeep in the path being laid by the tank's left track and kept his eyes on the back of the tank. The right tires had to make their own way. I wasn't sure this was going to work. Davis and the jeep struggled; I kept the mike in my hand so we could alert the TC if we got stuck.

The wide blades of grass were slapping the jeep on the passenger side and making scraping noises on the bottom of the jeep. I was concerned that the undercarriage or exhaust system would be destroyed. This was not something that had been covered in our driving training back at Fort Sill.

Finally the tank slowed again and climbed up a six-foot berm and made a hard left turn. We followed and found ourselves on a sort of a road. We crept down the road for maybe a hundred yards and the tank stopped and idled, buttoned up.

We were in "Indian Country" – territory controlled by the VC and we were sitting still. The tank was buttoned up with the crew behind some serious armor; the jeep was wide open.

My mind ran the words, "the valley of the shadow of death..." from the 23rd Psalm so I prayed the entire prayer to myself.

The tank had two radios and was communicating with someone else, we supposed. I keyed the mike, "Yellow Cat 67 this is Station Break 44, over."

Nothing.

The tank and the jeep were idling and making enough noise for any gook within a few hundred yards to easily find us. Davis and I each had our M16s in our hands, a round loaded in the chamber, the safety off and our fingers on the triggers.

"Station Break 44, this is Yellow Cat 67, over."

The fact that the tank was still buttoned up was a bit troubling. I would have felt better if the TC had stuck his head up out of the hatch. "This is Break 44, over."

"Okay, Dogies, this is your Delta Zulu. Some grunts are on their way; wait here."

The tank's engine revved up, the beast lurched back on its haunches and then dove forward, made a hard right, went down the berm, made another hard right turn and passed us on our right side as it made its way back in the direction we had come.

Then the radio came alive again, "Good luck."

It seemed like a half hour but it was probably only a few minutes when we saw silhouettes coming up from the berm on our left. We needed to quickly determine if these were the grunts we had been promised or the bad guys.

The heads appeared to have steel pots on them – a good sign. They were moving slowly and then went back down the berm – a bad sign. *"Did the NVA have steel pots?"* I wondered.

Davis had a clear shot from his position on the left side; if a party broke out I would need to dismount and fire across the hood.

A voice came up from the berm right beside Davis. "Doggies?"

"Gyreenes?" Davis answered. "Gyreenes" was an affectionate term for Marines – it was supposedly the sound of shit hitting the fan.

Four grunts came up to the jeep; one a sergeant. They had followed the tank's instructions but arrived at the road a few yards ahead of the jeep. They knew better than to walk on the road since it could have been mined and it would expose them to any VC nearby, so they had gone back down the berm and made their way to where we were.

The sergeant spoke softly.

"Follow us. We're camped by the river over there," and he pointed in the direction of meaningless elephant grass, "but there's a sniper taking shots at us. I'll lead you in behind the tree line. If he hears you he may take some shots at you."

The grunts went back down the berm. Davis backed up the jeep to have a straighter shot at the berm and we followed the grunts. We quickly cleared the elephant grass and were driving on what had been some kind of farmland. It was rough but much easier to negotiate than the grass.

There were numerous craters, the result of previous shelling by artillery and mortars. We could not see the holes in the dark and they could damage the jeep so I got out and hooked my flashlight to my back pocket. Military flashlights are L-shaped so the light comes out at a right angle from the body. Clipping it on my pocket would cause it to shine backwards. We had red lens on the flashlights since red light waves do not travel as far as other colors. Davis would follow the red light and I would take a circuitous route around the craters while keeping an eye on the grunts.

The noise from the straining jeep engine should have attracted the attention of any enemy in the area.

From the tree line we could see the river. "Charlie's in that general area", the sergeant said as he pointed to a clump of trees on the opposite side of the river. "He's not very good but he keeps us from getting water." The river water would have been used for shaving and bathing.

There were another dozen or so Marines sitting with us in the trees. Davis and I walked around and found a thicket where we could set up the light and have it partially camouflaged. We would unsuccessfully use the infrared to try and find the sniper.

Just before daybreak, we moved the jeep back into the trees so Charlie would not know where it was. Either I had missed him or he had taken the night off.

We broke out some C-Rats, set up the cots and called it a night. It had been a long one and we were bushed.

The small trees afforded little shade so we were awake after a few hours. I rolled over and looked down at the ground where I had put my boots and saw an unexploded 80MM mortar shell. It could go off at any time, especially if it was disturbed. When we had set up the night before it would have been easy for either of us to have stepped on it or kicked it.

Somehow in the darkness we had been spared again.

We carefully moved the jeep and all of our gear to a safer spot.

During the day the grunts filled us in. They had been there for several days running patrols in the area and finding various signs of possible NVA activity. That was not good news; the NVA were supposed to be on the other side of the river.

The sniper was their primary concern. I think it was mostly an ego thing. How could some VC yokel hold a squad of American Marines at bay?

We came up with a plan to move the jeep to the edge of the tree line at dusk, immediately scan with infrared and see if we could catch him coming to work.

It didn't work.

As far as I know he lived to a ripe old age because the next morning the squad of grunts was ordered to move out and we were not staying behind by ourselves. I radioed my base camp and asked where we were supposed to go. They did not have a clue; they did not even know the grunts were leaving. The coordination between the Marines in the field and the Marines in the rear was bad enough; the coordination between the Doggies and the Jarheads in the rear was even worse.

Davis and I had the jeep packed up and ready to move. All we needed to know was where. In one of my communications with base camp I learned that there was a field FDC set up near a burned-out school house that was noted on my map. It was probably an hour away so we decided that if no orders came we would go there since it would be relatively secure.

It was creepy sitting in the trees with no one else around.

We heard the Pig about the same time the radio came alive.

A Pig was a lightly armored, tracked vehicle with three 105 re-coilless rifles on each side. It was another vehicle that the Marines –

and no one else – used. The track gave it the ability to travel over rough terrain and the lighter weight allowed it to go places where a tank would bog down or crush the road or bridge under it.

The downside was that the recoilless rifles had to be loaded from outside the vehicle which would expose the loader to enemy fire. Also, the recoilless rifles were not as accurate as other weapons like the cannon on the tank. After six rounds were fired, someone had to go outside and reload the guns.

The radio message was that we would be escorted to another location farther upstream on the same river and the pig would be our escort.

Following the pig was easier than following the tank. First of all, it was daylight and secondly, the pig moved more slowly. After a couple of hours we arrived at a simple encampment on a flood plain beside the river.

A squad of grunts had been there for a couple of days and had observed some activity on the other side of the river. They had been joined by other units for a few hours at a time or overnight and those units included ARVN squads for whom there was little respect.

Since there was no cover – no trees or undergrowth, Davis and I decided to dig a hole for him to stand in while manning the machine gun. The shovel strapped to the side of the jeep and the soft ground of the flood plain would make this an easier task than it might have seemed.

This was the hole that Davis would find filled with "brave" ARVN grunts when enemy soldiers were spotted on the other side of the river. After Davis pulled them out they decided to go "fight" somewhere else.

We were less than 100 feet from the riverbank and the river was maybe forty yards wide so the Indian Country on the other side was not that far away. The vegetation on the other side was completely different. It was lush with plants and trees so we could not see more than a few feet from the river's edge on that side. That gave the enemy a distinct advantage and we all knew it. They had cover.

We ran missions that night with no results. The next morning we buttoned things up as well as we could, set up the cots, ate some C's and went to sleep.

We were awakened by some nearby commotion. When I opened my eyes I was facing the ground and saw black tennis shoes. The better-equipped Viet Cong wore black tennis shoes. What had happened?

I tried to gather my thoughts while pretending to be asleep. Where was my rifle? How quickly could I grab it? Where was Davis? How many were there?

I heard laughter and some chatter in Vietnamese.

I waited and then heard some Marines talking softly. If the VC had overwhelmed them would they be talking like that? No. Besides, no Marine unit would allow himself to be taken without a fight and the fight would have been noisy.

I rose up, saw that the tennis shoes belonged to ARVNS and my fear turned to anger. We had only been asleep for a couple of hours and now the adrenaline would keep us from getting any more. Davis was pulling on his shirt; I began pulling on my boots.

As soon as I sat up two ARVNS sat on my cot with me. They were all about comfort and prestige. They wanted to be seen with and respected by the American troops. The problem was they seemed to habitually do all the things that made them unappealing to us.

Another night at this position came and went with no activity. In fact, the jungle was so thick on the other side of the river that a brigade of enemy soldiers could have been having a convention and we would not know it.

Shortly after the sun came up the grunts supporting us were ordered to move out. Once again I got on the radio and asked where we were supposed to move; we were not staying where we were.

It took an hour or so and finally the answer came back. Operation Arizona was over. We were to meet up with our lieutenant and Lindsey at a burned-out schoolhouse. Another Pig would escort us and I was given their call sign and frequency.

I raised the Pig and found out where they were. We agreed on a rendezvous spot not far from where we were. Actually, the Pig crew had no idea who we were and initially insisted that we come to where they were. I had to hold firm and demand they come our direction. I told the TC on the Pig that I would make it worth his while.

The spot was based on a clue I had gotten from one of the grunts who had been supporting us. He said it was a massive watermelon patch.

As we drove to the spot on the map we came across some locals who had some of the black market soft drinks from the docks at DaNang. They sold each of us a Diet Cola for one dollar each when they were ten cents at the PX. Then they asked if we wanted ice.

Wow. Ice would be great in this heat. A papa-san unrolled a piece of burlap and showed us a block of ice four inches by four inches by six inches. The water used for the ice was brown and had visible strings, hair and other debris in it. Still, we would be able to rub our soft drinks against it and cool them down. "How much?" Davis acted uninterested. "Five dollah."

Davis was a good haggler but the peasant would not budge. So, we paid five dollars for the ugly block of ice but it did help cool the drinks.

We drove off and passed a shed full of bags of rice. We had been indoctrinated at Fort Sill and on the troop ship that the reason we were in South Vietnam was that it was the breadbasket of Southeast Asia. If South Vietnam fell, the story went, communism would flourish because they would be able to feed the people.

Printed on the bottom of the rice bags was, "GROWN IN THE USA".

These people could not even feed themselves and depended on American rice. So, what were we fighting for?

When we arrived at the south side of the watermelon patch we could see the Pig on a hillside not too far away, slowly making its way to where we were.

Davis and I helped ourselves to enough watermelons to serve ourselves, Lindsey and the lieutenant.

The Pig stopped on the other side of the patch and since we would be heading out that way Davis and I drove around the patch to where they were.

The three Pig crewmen were all brothers. When they saw the patch they began throwing melons in the Pig. The TC of the Pig gave me a big smile and a thumbs-up. Fresh fruit was a rare treat.

The Pig crew escorted us to the rendezvous point, the old schoolhouse, and never slowed down. We turned into the school-yard and found the others from G Battery.

The lieutenant and his driver, in clean, starched uniforms were there talking to Lindsey and his driver/gunner who looked like hell warmed over. We joined them and the four warriors from Operation Arizona made the two men from the rear look even more out of place.

With a big smile, the lieutenant handed each of us an ice cold Coke. We had not seen Coca-Colas in a long time and we almost never saw ice or anything cold. Today we had seen them twice.

Apparently it was a reward for enduring Operation Arizona for which G Battery of the 29th Field Artillery would receive a Unit Commendation. The lieutenant and his driver would now be able to wear a blue campaign ribbon framed in gold on their uniforms when they went home. In fact, everyone in G Battery would now be authorized to wear the ribbon. So would we, of course, and we each got a Coca-Cola (like they had every day).

I surprised them all with watermelon. We sliced them with our bayonets – never mind a little debris on the melon rind – and passed them around.

While all of this was going on, a few yards away a Canadian correspondent had been interviewing some Marines. He would have them enact a firefight while he "reported from the front lines". They all stood up and the correspondent showed each of them where and how they should crouch down. A Canadian cameraman lifted his camera to his shoulder and the "firefight" began.

First, one Marine ran in the direction of a hooch whose roof was visible above the trees. Then a second Marine followed, both firing their rifles in the direction of the hooch.

Apparently this was not good enough so the Marines were brought back, engaged in a discussion and the "firefight" was on again.

This time the correspondent crouched in front of the camera with the Marines "attacking" behind him and spoke into his microphone. Then the Marines began charging the hooch again.

This was too good. Lindsey grabbed his movie camera and began his shoot with Davis and I eating watermelon and drinking Coca-Cola. Then he panned around to a "vicious firefight" and "brave correspondent" and continued panning until he had the others in our party eating watermelon and drinking Coca-Colas.

If I had learned later that the correspondent had been awarded a prize for journalism I would have toasted him with a Coca-Cola.

The footage that Lindsey shot never made it home to the States.

We were debriefed and headed back to our respective hills.

Back on Hill 55 Davis and I would be able to take the first shower in several days and we would both take the night off and sleep a deep sleep in the comfort and safety of Hill 55.

My sleep would be interrupted by a pesky toothache.

## **P.T.S.D.**

*Operation Arizona followed the monsoon weather and reminded us that no matter how bad things were, they could always be worse. Moving around in unfamiliar territory at night, being escorted by people we did not know and heading to an unknown location was, indeed, stressful. We were learning that we could not depend on anyone. The icing on the cake came when we saw the artificial message that was being created for the folks back home. Not only did they not know what we are facing every day, they were being told a story that did not reflect reality. We knew a little about the war protestors, even though most of that information was censored from us. We thought our families were behind us and what we were doing but they weren't - mainly because they did not know what was really going on.*

# CHAPTER ELEVEN

## Toothache

Hill 55, Month Six, 120 Days to Go

Despite the quality work of the dentist back at Fort Sill, a persistent toothache was too much for me to manage with aspirin. So one morning I radioed in the sit rep and included the fact that I needed to see a dentist. They would need to bring out a replacement for a day or two while I was out and Martin took the leadership role.

On the main road back in the rear, not too far from our base camp, there was a Marine medical complex. Any dental care would be there. A three-quarter-ton truck came out to the hill and dropped off a rookie soldier I did not know. I took his place in the truck and the driver and I began the trip back.

When we reached the medical unit, there were some pretty decent tents and hooches for the officers and some lesser ones for us enlisted men. The driver let me out and I went to find a dentist.

I found him. He had recently graduated from dental school and been immediately inducted into the Navy and attached to a Marine division. His "office" was probably not what he had imagined it would be when he made the decision to enroll in dental college. It was an eight-man tent with a field drill, table and sterilizer. There was no chair and no dental assistant. It was just him, his portable drill and a few tools.

Someone had fashioned a dental chair out of artillery shell boxes. I sat on one, leaned back on another and he went to work while sitting on a crate. I was dirty but not as dirty as I would have been if the trip had been made in a jeep rather than a truck. He was used to seeing grungy troops, I surmised.

In short order he leaned back and said, "You need a root canal."

All I had ever heard about root canals was that I never wanted to have one.

He would be working without the benefit of an assistant or an x-ray.

He went to find some anesthesia and returned with some more bad news. He only had one injection left and a procedure like this usually required three. He would do the best he could and offered the first of many apologies for the "discomfort", a word they taught in dental school.

To say it was painful would be a huge understatement.

The tears running down my cheeks caused him to apologize frequently but he kept at his trade.

He began reaming out the tooth with increasingly larger files. As he reached for each new file he would say, "Almost there," or "Almost done." After using his largest file he sat, held the file in his hand, stared at it and said he still had a ways to go and needed an even larger one.

The pain now was as close to unbearable as I have ever experienced.

He leaned back on his crate again and said, "I need a larger file."

He looked in the direction of the officer's medical facilities and wrote something on a piece of paper and handed it to me. "You'll have to go up there and get one."

He gave me detailed instructions on exactly which hooch I was to go to and what to say. With the pain so intense I could not even focus my eyes, I climbed out of the chair, put on my pistol belt, picked up my rifle and began the walk up the hill.

The dentist facility there was different. There were stateside chairs, the types of lamps that were in dentists' offices back home and no shortage of corpsmen running around as assistants. Maybe I should have gone to OCS after all.

I handed the note to the first dentist I saw. He read it and looked at me with a look I had come to recognize. It was the look one human gives another when they see the other person suffering. I'm sure that look had been on my face when I watched wounded and dying Americans. We just cannot help it.

It did not feel good.

The dentist disappeared and returned with a rolled up paper towel. I assumed the needed tool was inside so I thanked him and began the walk back to the first dentist.

Once the procedure was completed, the young dentist handed me a bottle of pills. Apparently the officers' dentist had some compassion for an Army enlisted man and had included the bottle with the larger file.

I popped a couple of the pills as I left the dentist and walked back to base camp, arriving in time for supper. I was hungry and had thought I would enjoy some cooked food as a departure from a steady diet of C's. Once in the mess tent the smell of the food, the pain in the mouth and the effects of the pill were taking their toll. I drank some iced tea and went to find an empty cot.

With my rifle and boots on the floor, I popped a few more pills and curled up to sleep. It was a useless endeavor. After tossing and turning, maybe sleeping for a few minutes at a time, I gave up.

It was dark outside but there were enough electric lights for me to easily find my way around. My night vision had been honed to the point that no light was necessary to move around after dark.

I pulled on my boots, slung the M16 over my shoulder and walked over to the day room. It was surreal. I knew there was a day room, of course, every unit has one. The day room is where soldiers go to unwind at the end of the day. It just had not occurred to me how the folks back in the rear spent their evenings.

G Battery's day room was a hooch with a bar, several tables and chairs and some games. The bar served beer and soft drinks. I bought a Coke, the only soft drink available at the time, and sat down just in time for a movie to begin.

I moved my chair for a better view and in doing so caught a glimpse of my boots and everyone else's. What a stark contrast. The other boots would have passed inspection stateside; mine looked like they belonged to a poor ditch digger. I was unaware of the level of deterioration that was taking place mentally and physically.

And I was the only one in the room with a rifle.

The film that night was two episodes of a popular television program, "Combat". The program followed the lives of some grunts in World War II. It did not bother me because it was so "Hollywood" that it did not seem the least bit authentic. In fact, it was almost laughable.

Several of the guys would write letters home after the movie and use scenes from the movie to report what *they* had been doing!

Once the almost-cold cola was gone I considered taking up alcohol to relieve the pain.

I knew a few of the guys and they asked a lot of questions about what went on out on Hill 55 but when they realized I was in no mood or shape to talk, they left me alone. I would later learn that Station Break 44 was an admired and respected unit.

The next day it was decided that I was not ready to return to Hill 55 so I would spend another day and night in base camp. During the day our Lieutenant came over and talked for a long time. He was curious about what we were doing, how we spent our nights, etc. He turned out to be a decent guy.

I spent some time with the radio operators in the radio bunker, a shipping container buried under a mountain of sandbags. We talked frequently on the radio with my morning sit reps and occasional need for help so it was nice to have a face-to-face chat with them. I completely missed the fact that they saw me as some kind of a GI Joe; one of the few in the battery who was actively involved in combat.

The last morning I walked up to the dentist, he put some finishing touches on the tooth and I made my way back to base camp. I had had enough of the rear and was ready to go back to Hill 55.

In a few short months my preference for a lifestyle had changed from what I had experienced at home to the relative comfort of Fort Belvoir, to now, the remote bunker on Hill 55. I no longer desired what I saw as the inane lifestyle of base camp. Even though they ate cooked food and slept at night, what they were accomplishing seemed to be relatively meaningless. Some were already faking their war records and others were complaining about the discomforts.

I had already become a different person. I was blind to most of the changes; I thought I was still me. But I wasn't. It seemed normal to work nights and sleep days. C-rats were a palatable daily diet. The radio operators were as much involved in the war as I was – or so I thought.

Others saw me differently from the way I saw myself. That should have been a flag for me, but it wasn't.

When I arrived back on Hill 55, I had the mail and some resupplies. I relieved the temporary fill-in and found him as anxious to return to base camp as Martin was to see him leave.

The next day the lieutenant came out to the hill with the platoon sergeant, had all of us line up and announced I was being promoted to Sergeant E-5. Draftees rarely made it beyond E-3, Private First Class; I had arrived in Nam as an E-4, Corporal, and was now making sergeant. It was referred to as a battlefield promotion.

Lindsey would receive the same promotion the same day. There was some reward for being in the heat of battle regularly as it turned out. For Lindsey and me it was the major jump in pay; the rank did not really amount to much for us.

The Marine Corps was not as generous with their promotions so it was not uncommon for the Marines supporting us to think

I was a lifer, a career Army soldier. Driving up to the daily briefing one afternoon a young Marine private saw my stripes and yelled "Lifer!" at me. I stopped the jeep, walked over to him and asked, "How long have you been in-country?" "Seven weeks," he answered. "And you're in for three?" The Marine enlistment was a minimum of three years.

He nodded not sure where this conversation was going. "In February I will have finished my two year hitch. You'll still be here when the gooks go home. Who's the real lifer?" With that I climbed back in the jeep and drove to the briefing.

Station Break 44 quickly fell back into our routine and Charlie fell back into his, throwing more frequent parties.

The morning sit reps were becoming more intense. We knew the VC were more active and we did not know why.

### THE LIEUTENANT COMES CALLING

Apparently the conversation with the lieutenant while I was back in the rear had triggered something in him. He and the platoon commander from another platoon, also a first lieutenant, decided to spend the night on Hill 55 to see what combat was like. Martin did not like the idea but I saw little harm in it.

Midafternoon the two officers showed up in a staff jeep driven by a private who had been out to the hill a few times delivering the mail. Since he knew the route he had been recruited and would sleep on my cot that night. The private would sleep in the bunker while the officers came out to finger five with Martin and me.

We had tipped off the tank crew that officers would be there but saw no reason for any of us to change anything we were doing.

After all, we had survived months on the finger; any changes could be catastrophic.

About dusk six or seven of us were standing around talking. The two officers, Martin, two or three members of the tank crew and I formed a circle.

As they talked, I realized how tired and worn Martin's uniform looked compared to the near-spotless officers' uniforms. I hoped the officers would not try and punish Martin for looking so shabby and then I realized my uniform looked about as bad. Our efforts were taking a toll on our clothing as well as on us.

Suddenly, the two lieutenants were standing by themselves. Martin had started the jeep, grabbed his steel pot and was manning the machine gun. The tank crew had the engine roaring and the turret moving. I was on the radio alerting the bridge and the communications bunker, "INCOMING!"

I was using a standard pair of binoculars scanning the riverbank looking for any sign of Charlie. I glanced over and saw the two officers still standing where we had been talking. Why weren't they hitting the ground? Before I could warn them, someone on the bridge fired a few rounds into the tree line and Martin matched them with a burst from the machine gun.

It was not until then that the officers hit the ground and crawled around reaching for their rifles. Neither of them had on a flack vest or a steel pot. When it is quiet in a combat zone it could be deceptive and perhaps that's why the Old Man thought as he did. He never experienced silence followed by an immediate firefight.

The inexperienced lieutenants had missed the clue that the party was starting. Since they outranked me, I had not suggested they wear their flack vests – shouldn't they have known to do that?

It was a brief party. After a few bursts of small arms and machine gun fire, we stopped and looked for Charlie. We gave it a few more minutes, decided he was just testing us and shut down the light and the tank. By then it was dark.

I radioed in a sit rep and began preparing my first cup of coffee.

The two officers came over to where I was. They were not only now wearing their flack vests, they had them zipped up. We did not close ours because it restricted our movement and it was hot. While it exposed part of our body to leave them open, we saw it as a worthwhile trade-off. They had on their steel pots and their complexion had changed.

"What happened, Sergeant Reaves?"

This was the first time I had seen the lieutenant unsure of himself. It was his first time in combat. Maybe there was a connection.

What had happened was that the rest of us had heard the "angry bee", the lieutenants had missed it.

When a small arms round is flying through the air it sounds like an angry bumble bee. The "Bzzzzzzt" sound trails the actual bullet since sound travels slower than the projectile. That is why people say you never hear the bullet that hits you.

While we were standing around talking, those of us who lived by the rules and signals of combat had heard it. The officers were listening to the conversation. Granted, it was a surreal world, one that we were accustomed to; one they were not. One minute you're standing and talking. The next you're in the heat of a firefight.

Charlie had been watching. He was always watching which was kind of creepy. Apparently when he saw two crisp uniforms among those of us who were looking ragged, he assumed they were important or at least special people. On this night he would attempt to take them out but he was not in the mood for a full-fledged firefight.

After popping a couple of rounds at the officers he must have decided to call it a night.

We talked about this while I drank my coffee. It was another surreal moment in modern warfare.

Combat Trophy

A lot of thought goes into the design of military equipment. The windshield on a jeep, for instance, is designed to fold down on the hood to make it easier to fire a rifle while riding in the vehicle. The windshield can be easily removed by two men to lighten the vehicle.

The windshield was made of two pieces of flat, tempered glass which were relatively easy to replace. The frame was designed with a ten inch metal panel below the glass to protect the occupants.

One night we were having a party on finger one. I had the white light on a hooch in the tree line where we had seen muzzle flashes. I knelt down beside the jeep to plot the coordinates on the map when I heard an unfamiliar noise. There was a "BLAP!" followed by an angry bee, "Bzzzt".

When the sun came up we found an AK47 bullet hole, in the windshield frame. The round had pierced the panel below the glass and spared us having to replace it. As I studied the location of the hole, I knelt down to the same position I had been in when the bullet hit.

It has missed my head by less than four inches. Even with the steel pot, the projectile would have done damage, probably fatal damage.

I had been spared again; another bullet dodged.

The sit rep that morning reported the damage to the vehicle. I was instructed to spot paint the windshield frame to keep it from rusting. That was supposed to be the end of it.

On our next trip to the rear for jeep servicing, the guys back in base camp circled around the jeep and examined the bullet hole. They put their fingers in the hole and had their pictures taken with it. All of that struck me as juvenile but then I was not like them. The buzz about the windshield was making the rounds at base camp; while the five of us were at the PX, supply tent and mess hall stocking up on supplies.

Back at base camp while the others were preparing the jeeps for the trip back to Hill 55 and hooking up the trailers, I made the mandatory visit to the orderly room to see if there were any instructions, demands or criticisms for me. I always hoped the Old Man would not be there and this day he was not. Corporal Clark chatted about a few mundane things, he gave me some insight into what the Captain was thinking and doing these days and that was that. No meddlesome messages this time.

The jeeps were lined up and ready to roll. Martin was behind the wheel, as usual, casually smoking a cigarette, as usual, and talking to one of his friends. I sat down in the right-hand seat in no particular hurry to leave.

That's when I noticed something was different. There was no hole in the windshield frame. Not only that, the frame looked like it had actually been waxed which was something we never did.

Martin saw me looking at the frame, turned his head towards me and said, "Captain Hayworth said we cannot have damaged equipment; it's unauthorized. They gave us a new windshield."

The new windshield looked like it had been waxed. The Old Man's driver regularly washed and waxed the Captain's jeep.

Then he pointed toward the maintenance tent. There a couple of mechanics were installing the "trophy" windshield on the Old Man's jeep. It was still on his jeep when I rotated home months later.

We headed back to Hill 55. As we left the city limits of DaNang we put on our steel pots, chambered a round in our M-16s and began making dust clouds.

Sergeant Dawkins Fires A Round – The Shot Heard Round the Hill

Our senior platoon sergeant was SGT Dawkins. Back at Fort Sill he had picked up the nickname The Hawk because of his profile. When viewed form the side, his head looked like a hawk.

After hearing the stories from Hill 55 and, especially, seeing how the lieutenants who had spent the night with us were being treated as seasoned combat veterans, he decided to come out and spend the night as well.

Martin refused to go out on finger five with him so Davis and I went. Martin did not trust him and saw him as dangerous in a firefight. It was about time for Martin to have a night off anyway.

Once on the finger, The Hawk kept his steel pot on his head the entire time. While Davis and I were talking with the tank crew

The Hawk laid down on the ground in the prone firing position pointing his M16 towards a rice paddy.

I did not think much about it. It was still light outside, we had not even positioned the jeep so nothing was going on.

Suddenly a shot rang out.

Of course everyone scrambled. In less than a minute the tank was running, Davis was on the machine gun having jumped over The Hawk to get there, start the jeep's engine and slide down behind the M60. I was on the radio and the Marines on the bridge were scrambling.

Quickly I learned that SGT Dawkins had fired the round. It may have been the only round he fired in Vietnam but it would reverberate enough to cause aggravation.

It did not take too long for everything to settle back down so I asked him why he fired. He said he had seen a Vietcong coming out of a cave, had shot him and seen him fall back inside. He would repeat this story many times back in base camp.

The problem was there were no caves around us.

The next morning before going to sleep I would have to report to the command bunker and be dressed down by Major Huffman. I would have to explain what happened to my platoon commander and, eventually, to the Old Man.

HELPLESS

Charlie was stepping up his game. The Marines decided to send out more listening posts which made our job close to impossible. During the daily briefings I would be shown where the

LURPS would set up, or at least where they were supposed to set up. Based on what I saw there was little room for using the searchlight; it would be too easy to illuminate them.

I told Martin that we would only be running the infrared that night.

The patrols of four to six men each walked out and across the bridge after dark. I watched them through the infrared binoculars until they disappeared in the tree line across the river. They would be equipped with their rifles, a few grenades and three types of flares. White flares would be used for illumination with the understanding that the flare would also illuminate their own position. A green flare would be used when they came back in; a green flare meant "I'm friendly; don't shoot." Finally, a red flare would be used if and only if they were being overrun and needed serious help.

The still quiet of the night was broken by a radio transmission. I was using the speaker on the jeep's radio, not the headset. "Pffft, Pffft, Pffft."

One of the patrols needed to communicate. One by one the communications bunker polled the units by call sign, asking if they needed to communicate. All were answered by, "Pffft, Pffft," the signal for "no". Finally, one responded "Pffft," yes.

I looked on my map and found where that particular listening post was supposed to be and showed the location to Martin. He slid down behind the machine gun and faced in that direction.

The comm bunker asked a series of questions that could be answered yes or no and we learned that a large number of enemy soldiers were close to the Lima Papa.

There was nothing we could do. Obviously we could not fire since we did not know their exact location and I was not about to turn on the white light. The infrared was showing me nothing.

Then a firefight broke out. We saw a few tracers followed by multiple rapid fire pops. Since only a few rounds were tracers, many bullets were fired that could not be seen. The firefight sounded like a string of firecrackers had been lit or like an ambitious popcorn popper.

We could see tracers going towards each other but we had no way of telling who was who. The comm bunker asked me if I could tell them anything but of course I couldn't.

The Lima Papa broke radio silence which was not a good sign. When the radio operator keyed his mike we would hear a distinctive pattern of rifle shots and then, a few seconds later, that same pattern would reach finger five.

He was desperate. In a loud whisper he told us they had taken casualties, were outnumbered and needed help.

None was coming because none was available.

The firefight continued. A white flare went up so we knew which of the two groups of shooters the LURPS were. I sent this information to the comm bunker but we still could not pinpoint exactly where the enemy was.

The firefight became one-sided; many rounds from one side and few from the other. A red flare went up, a few more rounds were fired and then silence.

The comm bunker tried in vain to raise someone on the radio.

Some time passed as the night became still and quiet. An oriental voice came on the radio, "Hello, G.I.!" That was followed by a laugh and then more silence. The gooks had our radio and would now be able to monitor everything that was said. Tomorrow we would move to another channel.

They also had a green flare which they would use at some point to fool some unsuspecting American troops into opening a gate and letting them in. After all, a green flare means "friendlies".

The bodies were recovered the next morning.

A couple of days later the personal belongings of each member of the patrol would be stuffed into their duffle bags and stored. It was not uncommon for some of the Marines to swap their boots for the ones going into storage. Resupply, after all, was spotty on Hill 55.

### P.T.S.D.

*The time in the rear taught me that there were two different Vietnam Wars – the rear and the field (there was no front). Had I understood the difference and been given a choice, I would probably have chosen the rear with three cooked meals each day and movies at night instead of firefights. Some resentment arose from this visit. The idea that there might have been an alternative to my situation on Hill 55 added to the stress. The people responsible for supporting us did not understand our situation and I did not want to spend time with them.*

# CHAPTER TWELVE

## Hearing From Home

Hill 55, Month Seven, 90 Days to Go

T he first level of "short-timer" was when the days left in country were less than 100. I had reached that point.

Nothing caries a higher priority for soldiers in combat than hearing from home. When the soldier is in training in the states, mail call is a time of excessive anticipation often followed by great disappointment. Not hearing from home can cause a warrior to wonder and worry.

For some reason, our base camp could not coordinate with the local Marine mail process so we relied on members of our own outfit to bring us our mail. The length of the dusty drive and the perceived potential for danger limited their willingness to come out to two or three times a week. For the soldier wondering what's going on with his wife, kids or girlfriend, days can be tormenting, especially when no letter arrives.

If our mail person knew we were a few days away from returning to the rear to service the jeeps, they would not come out.

For them, what were a few more days? Never mind they had daily mail calls.

When someone received a "Dear John" letter, word would spread and we would all know to keep a watchful eye on them. They could easily be in a mood to harm themselves or others.

If we were sending in situation reports with regular enemy engagement, they would not come out as often for fear of being attacked. The enemy attacked at night, rarely in the day time so there was little danger of a ¾ ton truck with a couple of enlisted men in the cab being hit.

Any excuse would do and hearing one of those excuses would almost be my undoing on my way out of Nam.

We could mail for free and all we needed was paper and envelopes. Those were not as plentiful as we would have liked so stocking up on stationary was a part of our agenda on our twice-monthly trips to the rear.

Another way we heard from home was the media. The military published a newspaper, *"The Stars and Stripes"*. The news articles were chosen and written by the military. Some potentially demotivating stories were watered down and others were omitted. However, our access to the traditional media was improving as time went by.

At first the stories and pictures of mass war protests were greeted with derision. As we read them and talked about them we would spitefully say, "Pussies!" "Cowards!" "Wait until we get home!"

The emotion changed as the reports continued to come in and we saw how many people were against the war we were reluctantly fighting. That had not happened before in American history to such a degree.

Bravado changed to uncertainty. Were we right?

Then it became personal. "Baby killers" was the worst for me. Yes, there are casualties in war at all levels, including babies. It happens. And, it hurts. The moniker implied that we were deliberately seeking out the weak and doing despicable things that we were not doing. We were painfully aware that the things we were doing were bad enough and that our hands were not really clean. So when words were spoken or written about innocent people being victims of the war, it hit close to home for us.

That is when uncertainty began to morph into despair for many of us. It was becoming obvious we were not viewed positively, let alone as heroes, for most of the folks back home.

## THE ONLY TIME I CRIED

The ¾-ton truck made its usually noisy arrival at the bunker around two in the afternoon. We had finally trained them not to come out to the hill in the morning because we were trying to get whatever sleep the day would offer us. So, they would eat lunch and then make their way out to the hill and leave as quickly as they could.

The truck usually had what we needed – or what they thought we needed or deserved - in the back under the canvas and a couple of privates in the front seat. They would have our precious mail in the front seat with them and we could not wait to dig into the envelopes.

When I heard the truck laboring up the rise leading to the bunker, I went out to greet them. Shortly the other members of Station Break 44 joined us.

SSGT Dawkins was in the right front seat so this would not be good news. "Captain Hayworth is setting some new rules."

A real leader supports the initiatives of their superiors; SSGT Dawkins was passing the buck with a "don't blame me" approach. *"New rules, fine",* I thought. He rattled off a list and I was surprised that most of it was a rehash of previous rules which we only obeyed when we knew we were being watched.

Then he dropped the bomb. The Old Man wanted us to obey the no-fire zone rules again. Hill 55 was now a free-fire zone and some of the parties had been pretty hot. Now we were under orders not to return fire when those around us were actively engaged in a firefight. The Old Man was back on his kick that there were no enemy combatants in our sector. Maybe he needed to see some of what we had seen or maybe even a few body bags would have changed his mind. But, I doubt it.

As the sergeant walked around to get back into the truck, the driver handed me the bundle of mail. This was more important to us than any resupply that had come out in the back of the truck.

As he handed the mail to me he said, "We actually forgot these and when I turned around to go back and get them sergeant Dawkins told me the mail could wait. I went back anyway and he was pretty pissed."

"Thanks, man," was all I could muster. SSGT Dawkins was supposed to be looking out for us but I learned over and over that he would easily throw any of us to the wolves to protect his rank and position in the Army. He was closing in on retirement and all he wanted to do was to draw his Army pension. Anything that threatened his exit was a threat he would attack.

What were we supposed to do? Our commanding officer had placed a no-fire order on us; the Marines on Hill 55 would not hesitate to use everything they had to eliminate the enemy.

Before reading my mail I would need to go to the command bunker.

At that time the senior officer was Major Huffman, a man I respected for many reasons including the months with the same three inch stub of a cigar in his mouth. He was gruff and fair – what more could we want?

His orderly was a Lance Corporal who was a little too clean cut so he must have been new to Nam. I asked for permission to speak to the major and the orderly disappeared into the major's quarters.

He returned and escorted me into a small chamber in the bunker where a single radioman was sitting with headphones and a magazine.

When the major entered the room I did not salute. In a combat zone we did not salute.

"I have a situation, Major," I began. "My Old, ah, my commanding officer has placed a no-fire order on us. I'm not sure what I'm supposed to do. I don't want my guys out where they cannot defend themselves but I don't want to park the jeeps either. What am I supposed to do?"

This was awkward. Here I was, an Army enlisted man asking a Marine officer what I was supposed to do about an order from an Army officer.

"Who's your CO?" the major barked. He was trying to determine if the "Little Prick" was still in charge of my unit. I could not tell if he was angry with me or the Old Man.

"Captain Hayworth, sir."

"What's his sign?"

"Station Break One."

"You're dismissed."

I drove back down to the bunker not knowing what was going on and decided to focus on my mail. Like most young men, I read the letters from my fiancé first and then opened the one from my mother.

My mother's letter opened with the line, "I hope this is the hardest letter I ever have to write..."

What an ominous opening. If there had been a death in my immediate family I would have been notified personally by someone from the rear. Or would I?

She went on to explain that my dog had died. Pee Wee, named after Pee Wee Reese the baseball legend, was old and had problems. But the fact that in the last days the dog had spent every day staring at the back door of the house where I usually came in was just too much. I lost it.

Fortunately I was alone.

An hour or so later the five members of Station Break 44 gathered at the bunker for dinner. The others broke out their C-Rations; I wasn't hungry.

Outside the radio on one of the jeeps crackled with "Station Break 44, Station Break 44 this is Stations Break Niner, over." That was the call sign of our command bunker back in the rear. The radios really were not powerful enough to operate from that distance but a newly-installed antenna back at base camp made the transmission barely understandable in the static.

I went outside and keyed the mike. "This is Break 44, over."

"Roger, Break 44, stand by."

Another voice came over the radio. It sounded like SSGT Dawkins but I could not be sure. Once he began a long rambling message about the no-fire restriction being lifted but we were still to fire only when fired upon and that should not be happening too often and we had better behave or else, I knew it was Dawkins.

Someone had gotten to the Old Man which was good news and bad. Would he now seek revenge? I had other things on my mind based on the letter from home.


SPORTS

Then there was the time I wrote home to my folks about how my request for a football or baseball had been answered. We were not getting any exercise other than going to the river and filling water cans and passing them up a ladder to fill our makeshift shower. So I requested something we could use to exercise like a football.

It took nearly two weeks but finally, on one trip out to the hill the ¾-ton truck lumbered up to the bunker with our "exercise equipment". It was a fresh, crisp box of dominos.

217

So I wrote home I told the story of how grateful and joyful we were that the folks in the rear would send us dominos. What a blessing!

I knew my father, a decorated World War II veteran, would recognize the sarcasm for what it was. This type of griping is as much a part of the Army as roll call. My mother, on the other hand, saw it as a great way to reward the troops and immediately went out and bought quantities of dominos.

My father stopped her from mailing them.

There was an issue in sending things home. Letters generally got through easily enough but packages were subject to inspection. After all, soldiers were not allowed to send home war souvenirs or any type of weapon. It was against regulations.

The problems would happen when one of us bought something at the PX. The prices for cameras and electronics were very low for the military and in Nam there was no sales tax. Some of the places we could go for R&R, like Japan, had even lower prices. So we would buy the stuff and ship it home.

While it did not happen a lot, it happened. Someone would send home a package of goods and some of the items would be missing when the box reached the States. The missing item was usually a camera or a tape recorder. The inspectors would not find weapons we should not be sending home but they would find goodies *they* would send home.

As we learned more and more about what was being reported on the nightly news and how it did not line up with what we were experiencing, we knew the fix was in but, of course, we did not know why. The war that the folks talked about in their letters was not what we were seeing and never was what we had read in the press.

News magazines made their way to us and occasionally some pages would be missing. Still, we knew enough to know about the war protesters and the declining support for the war. Since the people we heard from directly were our family and friends, our perspective was that most people supported us and only a few were detractors.

My fiancé was writing about wedding plans. At first it was a nice diversion. Later it just became another source of decisions I needed to make about things I could not understand. I tried to be supportive. She could not support me because she could not begin to understand what I was experiencing even if I had taken the time to tell her about it – which I hadn't.

Thoughts and emotions had to be buttoned up like the hatches on a tank, I thought.

I tried to arrange for ushers by writing to some guys and was disappointed that they could not find the time to write back so I would have to write again. And again.

There were days when eloping seemed to be the better option and even more days when staying single seemed preferable. I could not trust my civilian self while I was immersed in the Sergeant Reaves Chuck instead of the civilian Chuck.

TOKYO

It was time for R&R. Married soldiers could go to Hawaii or Australia and meet their wives there. Single guys like me left those slots open for the married warriors. Thailand was an option but it seemed too much like Nam and too close. I chose Tokyo.

To prepare for my trip I pulled out my duffle bag from under my cot and dug deep to find my dress uniform. The military would provide transport but I had to be in uniform and I could not wear fatigues.

The bag had not been opened very often since arriving on Hill 55 and then only to store something near the top. My dress uniform would be near the bottom where I had packed it back at Fort Sill months earlier..

When I pulled out my dress shoes they appeared to have green sponges in them. It turned out to be mildew, the thickest I have seen. After washing them out, I put them in the sun to dry, hung the uniform coat, pants and shirt on nails to air out and began planning for some time away.

A three-quarter ton truck came out to the hill, dropped off a replacement and carried me back to base camp. A trip to the PX netted me a couple of shirts and slacks and a travel bag. I was good to go.

The military made the trip easy. All I had to do was sign some papers covered in military gibberish and I would be handed a plane ticket and some instructions. The plane would be a military transport that would take a load of us to Osaka. From there a military bus would take us to a military R&R center at Camp Zama near Tokyo.

All of this was covered by the military as were the sleeping quarters and meals at the center.

In fact, Camp Zama even had a wonderful golf course and one of the guys I met was trying to become a golf pro and asked me to play golf with him. I told him that I was a lousy player and he said the rules required no less than two players so he needed anyone who would just walk the course with him. We signed out some clubs and for a few hours I was in a world of serene green grass, manicured grounds, lavish buildings and smiling Asian people.

The R&R center also had a barber shop run by a husband and wife team. He cut hair, she did manicures and neck massages. I had never experienced a real neck massage. The Vietnamese barbers on Hill 55 would pop our necks at the end of our haircuts but this was completely different from anything I had ever experienced. I could feel the tension leaving in waves. It was remarkable.

Standing behind me and chattering in broken, limited English, she asked the usual questions like where I was from, etc.

Then she pointed to my hands which were resting palms-down on the arm of the chair. She came around so I could see her face and I saw a worried look. As she pointed to my hands she made a sound like an explosion while spreading her arms palm up. I was puzzled until I looked at my hands and saw what a mess they were with bruises, cuts and scars.

She was asking how my hands got that way. I shrugged my shoulders.

Some people received Purple Hearts for similar – and lesser – wounds, something that never crossed the minds of people on Hill 55.

Once we left the R&R center we were on our own. On my third day I mustered the nerve to take off and see the city. It was amazing. For someone who had limited travel experience this was another world entirely. I had grown up in the Atlanta area and knew how to navigate a large city but this was way beyond any experiences in my past.

The bus dropped me off near the Ginza and even in the morning sun the neon lights made a spectacular show. The streets were crowded and everyone seemed to be in a hurry and determined to be somewhere for some reason. I just stood and tried to take it all in.

The store windows were like an amusement park with so many new things to see. A few blocks away the Sony building stood tall and inviting so I made my way there in no particular hurry.

The building was on a corner and had display windows on both streets. Inside, there was a staircase that went up floor after floor with more displays. I was in another world.

One display was a new technology at the time called nixie tubes. These were vacuum tubes with ten elements inside and each element was shaped like a number. When voltage was applied to a certain element, it would glow and the number could be seen. This was a major breakthrough in technology. Now a single device could display any number! This would lead to revolutionary new designs in calculators, displays and computers. I stared transfixed at the incredible little devices which are now so obsolete they cannot be found.

Another display was an electronic pipe organ, a precursor of the keyboards used now. What made this one extraordinary was that it had actual pipes just like you would see in a large church or cathedral only the pipes were made of bamboo.

Bamboo was the material of hooches and punji pits and here it was automatically making beautiful music every half hour.

I accomplished two of my three objectives while on R&R: 1) Gifts for the folks back home, 2) Buy my first car using the special program set up for military vets returning to the States and, 3) Find some replacement china for my mother's "good dishes". Her Sunday china was Noritake, was out of production and I was determined to find some pieces for her but I failed on that one.

Gifts would come from the department store off the Ginza, Tokyo's equivalent of Macy's. The store was immaculate, sparsely stocked compared to what I had seen in the five-and-dimes back home where every square inch was stocked in merchandise. The store was staffed with well-dressed, smiling and helpful people. A few signs in English and a helpful English-language pamphlet were lifesavers.

First I would buy a pearl necklace for my fiancé. The prices were excellent especially with the conversion rate with the dollar.

Next I would need to go up several floors to find something for my mom and dad and the only options were stairs and an attendant-operated elevator. I stepped causally into the elevator, went up a floor and was slammed to the back by a mob of middle-aged Japanese women talking ninety miles an hour. They were the most aggressive shoppers on the planet and they were making their way floor to floor, sale to sale.

The next floor was ladies underwear and as soon as the elevator doors opened they were out and surrounding a table four or five deep. The table appeared to have a "SALE" sign on it. The ladies closest to the table would look at an item and if they did not want it would toss it in the air so the women behind them cold get a look. The ladies farther back would grab the item and if they did not want it toss it to the ones behind them.

I stood in the elevator and watched. What a show. Before the doors could close, this mob had surrounded the table and created a volcano of erupting women's underwear all the while jabbering incessantly.

When I found something I wanted to buy, I would hold out my supply of Yen and let the clerk count out the amount needed. They were honest people who laughed and smiled during these transactions.

With my shopping successfully completed, I made my way back to the street to forage for lunch. I found an eatery with the kind of menu I wanted: one with pictures. I went in, sat down, pointed and ate. No one there spoke English and none was needed.

With my confidence building and my purchases neatly wrapped and tucked in a sturdy shopping bag, I began exploring the city, determined to stay until dark, see the lights and make my way back to the R&R center.

Several times some sleazy-looking man would offer to "show me good time" because they "know nice place". I had no intention of visiting their nice place. Being a non-Asian made me a target for these folks; I guess every society has their share of people like that.

Sipping hot tea and watching the neon lights come even more alive as the sun began to set was how I ended my day downtown. I would need a ride back to the bus depot and decided to take a taxi. I had only recently learned how to use a taxi in my Fort Belvoir days so I was new to the art.

At a taxi stand nearby I showed the driver my bus ticket, he smiled, bowed slightly and I climbed in the cab. This was not like any cab I had seen in America. Behind my head was a knitted doily, on the floor was a pair of slippers and in the middle of the back seat was a basket of fruit and hard candy.

I thought this was a genteel and civilized way to travel until the driver took off. He apparently had little use for the brake pedal and preferred, instead, the artful use of his horn. There were times he would squeeze the vehicle in places it did not seem it would fit.

Asians, as a rule, are quiet and polite people who rarely demonstrate a level of panic. This was one of those rare times. From the driver hunched over the steering wheel to the wide-eyed pedestrians in the crosswalks, I saw a different side to the docile stereotype.

The only Japanese words I knew were Kamikaze and Hari Kari and, for a moment at least, I thought I might have the opportunity to use either or both of them.

Safely back at the R&R center, the next day was spent ordering a new car. There was a program for certain military personnel that allowed us special pricing and no sales tax for cars to be delivered to certain dealerships in the States. Fortunately I qualified and one of the dealerships was in the Atlanta area.

I had never owned a car before. So my very first automobile would be a brand new Buick LeSabre coupe, Teal Mist Blue with a black vinyl top and air conditioning. If all went well it would be waiting for me when I got home.

In high school I had inherited primary use of the family's 1951 Henry J. At some point in his career, Henry J. Kaiser decided to expand his aluminum empire and manufacture automobiles. His family-friendly compact was the Henry J. It was mostly aluminum which gave it the crash protection of a pie pan. The federal standards were lower in those days. The all-aluminum, four-cylinder "Supersonic" engine gave it enough power to go from zero to sixty in less than an hour. It was sold through the Sears and Roebuck Catalog.

My parents had bought it from some members of our church for $220 and it was one of their best investments from an ROI point of view. The car had been wrecked on three sides – people either ran into us or, on one of the frequent brake failures, we ran into someone else. Either way, we took the insurance money, spent it on food and clothing and let the car fend for itself.

One afternoon my mother decided to correct some of the body damage. She had my sister and I lean into the opened right-hand door while she jabbed it from the inside with a mop. Most of the damage to that door was repaired when the giant dent popped back out. It was replaced a few months later with a crease that was beyond the repair capabilities of a mop.

As the rust spread across the Henry J, my mother, who would paint anything, undertook painting the car turquoise, a popular color at the time. Visible brush strokes were not the worst results of her efforts even though a man at the gas station asked if it had been painted with a pine cone.

What made the paint job less than stellar was the fact that she ran out of paint and the second can was not exactly the same shade.

The Henry J was my high school chick magnet.

Fortunately, my enterprising father talked a man into painting the car for the price of the paint and a six-pack. The results indicated that he probably bought the six-pack first. No attempt was made to remove any of the dents or to waste sandpaper on the old finish.

I would learn to make parts for the car since none were available. A flexible fuel line, for instance, began with a Chevrolet fuel line, an American Motors fitting on one end and a plumbing fitting from the hardware store on the other.

From these humble beginnings I would be elevated to a brand new Buick as my first car.

The appointment with the Japanese man responsible for handling my purchase was another new experience. Since most of my pay was going home, I had some strong savings for a down payment. He and I chatted for a few minutes and then he got down to business.

I said, "Buick," and he pulled out the Buick file. I said, "LeSabre," and out came the beautiful, full color brochure. He pulled out a checklist of available options and an abacus. With his finger on the "Base Price" number, he moved the beads on the abacus with lightning speed. He had obviously done this before.

"Transmission?"

"Automatic."

Beads flew back and forth on the abacus. "Color?"

"Teal Mist Blue with a black vinyl top."

"Teal Mist," he said, moving more beads, "Vinyl top," and the beads continued moving.

In about the time it takes to say, "Made in Japan," he had run the numbers and showed me the total which was about what I had expected. There was no negotiating. If the price needed to be lowered, they only way would have been to downgrade the car. The order was placed.

That afternoon I took my purchases from the day before to the military post office and shipped them home, then signed up for a three-minute phone call home. We were entitled to one and I would use it to call my fiancé. The call would be set up by HAM Radio operators who volunteered their time and capabilities for people they did not know. God bless them.

It was a complex process but finally the call was established and I talked with her. I cannot remember the conversation, what was said or how it was said. I just remember hanging up and thinking the marriage would not be a good idea. I was not the same person who had proposed and she was probably not the person I had proposed to.

Less than happy, I spent the last two days of R&R resting, reading, relaxing and compartmentalizing – something I was learning to do easily.

Thanksgiving

I had convinced myself that I would be home for Christmas and was hoping I would be home for Thanksgiving as well. If I had to spend one holiday in Nam of course I would choose Thanksgiving.

We worked out an arrangement with the tank crew to have our dinner in their newly-acquired hooch which had electricity and an electric frying pan. Plans were made. We would all gather what we could for the feast and meet early that afternoon for the festivities. In the meantime we would all forage for whatever contribution we could make to the menu.

We scheduled our next trip to the rear accordingly and Martin and I made our usual foray to the Marine mess tent where he was unusually adept at procuring some goodies for the feast. The mess tent had gotten some specialty items for the holiday and we assumed we would share in those. So we added a number ten can of sweet potatoes, ready to eat, and a loaf of white bread.

The tank crew had also been successful and had a large can of spam which, when fried, tasted like, well, fried spam. There was a menagerie of canned vegetables and some kind of canned dessert that was a cross between pudding, cake and Jell-O. Still, it wasn't C-Rations and we were thankful.

The feast was remarkable at the time; disgusting in retrospect. Young bodies can manage diets like that.

Afterwards, Martin and I went to finger five with the tank crew while the other team went to the north side of the hill that night. We were warned in the briefing that the enemy often uses holidays to attack but they didn't. It was a quiet night except for the sounds of our stomachs digesting the strange food.

## P.T.S.D.

*There was a stark disconnect between home and Nam. It was difficult for my mind to embrace both worlds at the same time. So I compartmentalized. Life and death were moving along at home, just as in Nam – but different somehow. Buick was building a wonderful automobile that would be waiting for me when I got home, even if my dog would not. During the day I would think about being at home and at night I would think about staying alive. Each firefight brought its own challenges. Sometimes during the day following a tough firefight the night before, it would occur to me that I might never see the Buick just as I would never see the dog again.*

# CHAPTER THIRTEEN
## I'll Be Home for Christmas

Hill 55, Month Seven, 60 Days to Go

There was an "Early Out" program. If a man in Nam was due to go back to school or to help the family farm harvest the crop, they could get out of Nam up to sixty days early. Most of us wanted out as soon as possible but few of us qualified under the rules of the program.

With a church full of people praying for me back home and with me praying for an early out, I was sure I would make it home by Christmas which was about forty days early.

Of course when the military is involved, nothing is ever simple.

Corporal Devereaux was our lieutenant's driver. He lived in base camp so he knew all of the rules and regulations and how to circumvent them. He was a good guy, one of us, even though his uniform was never dirty or torn and his jeep was waxed.

He applied for winter quarter at LaSalle University for the sole purpose of gaining an Early Out. He completed the reams of paperwork, including all of the required documents from the university, and submitted them to the First Sergeant.

The First Sergeant, MSGT Layton, was a career man who did not like programs like the Early Out. He did not, however, mind "creative soldiering" as he demonstrated when we were on bivouac at Fort Sill and Lindsey and I had to face him and Clark in a pinochle battle. He was just the opposite of the Old Man: he did not care for people in Devereaux's position but did like Lindsey and me.

The First Sergeant went through the paperwork, looked at Devereaux and said, "It won't be approved."

"Why?" Devereaux asked.

"You'll see."

It took over a week for the paperwork to come back rejected. It turned out that the hundred-year-old school did not specifically state in its acceptance letter that prestigious LaSalle University was accredited.

Devereaux wrote another letter to the Dean of Admissions, received another letter from the university and resubmitted the paperwork.

"Won't go." MSGT Layton said without looking up from the package.

"Why? Tell me what I need to do!" Devereaux was getting desperate. Time was running out and he was still stuck in limbo.

Just over a week later the rejected paperwork was returned with the explanation that the school had not specifically stated that Devereaux was enrolling in a four-year study to earn a degree for his chosen profession.

Devereaux wrote the Dean of Admissions again. This time he received a large packet with the most detailed possible explanation that went on for pages and explained the University's credentials, Devereaux's educational program and anything else the military could possibly want, or so he thought. There was a separate letter addressed to Devereaux where the Dean explained that he, too, had been in the Army and understood these things.

With the enlarged stack of papers, Devereaux made his third trip to the First Sergeant and heard the now familiar, "It won't go." More than a week later he would learn why.

The Dean had not signed the letter for the Army. He had signed the letter to Devereaux, but not the official letter.

When Devereaux protested that the letter had been written on embossed University letterhead with gold foil, the master sergeant had said, "You could have forged that."

"If I had gone to the trouble to forge embossed letterhead wouldn't I have forged the signature?"

Logic has no place in the Army; ask any former soldier.

At that time, the Army had a Command Sergeant Major. Not only was this the highest NCO rank, it was very rare and so respected that officers below General Grade would typically obey a Command Sergeant Major. Most of us had only seen the rank illustrated in books; none of us had ever seen one and thought we never would.

A couple of days after Devereaux's last visit with the First Sergeant, a shiny jeep drove into base camp. This one stood out. It had a rank insignia on the front bumper and two starched soldiers in their green dress uniforms in the front seats. The driver was a Staff Sergeant, not the usual private or corporal. The man in the right seat dismounted smartly and displayed a chest full of ribbons.

On his sleeve were the stripes of a Command Sergeant Major.

Above his right pocket was his name tag. It read simply, "DEVEREAUX".

In all the time we had known him Corporal Devereaux had never mentioned his brother, the Command Sergeant Major. This was by design; he did not want preferential treatment.

Somehow the paperwork for Devereaux's Early Out was processed in about the amount of time it took for him to pack and he left with his brother in the fancy jeep that afternoon.

He was home for Christmas.

BACK ON HILL 55

December and January were busy months for us. There were constant parties – sometimes several in a single night which was unusual. We would learn later that the North Vietnamese Army was bringing in massive ordinance in preparation for the Tet Offensive.

Their weaponry began in North Vietnam, came down the Ho Chi Minh Trail into Laos, and then turned in toward DaNang just south of Hill 55. Leaving North Vietnam they would be using trucks and other modern vehicles. By the time they were near us they were using crude wagons and carts with no motors. After all, we would have heard the engines.

These shipments took weeks or months. The idea that the enemy in Vietnam was a seat-of-the-pants army simply was not true. They were organized and were as patient as they were diabolical.

During Tet they would launch rockets from the valley on the north side of the hill. Since the rockets were being brought in on the south side of the hill they and needed to be moved to the north side, so they would engage us in a firefight in one place while they moved the rockets around to another area.

We thought it was an attack; we did not know it was primarily a diversion. After all, when you're being hit with small arms fire, mortars and grenades, it feels like an attack.

When the party started, it was all hands on deck. We pointed everything we had towards the south side of the hill as we always did and engaged as well as we could in the dark.

The problem here was that was what "we always did". Guerilla warfare succeeds when the conventional fighters do conventional things. Guerillas capitalize on that.

During one of the late night/early morning firefights there was a disturbance behind us on the north side of finger five. Nothing ever happened on the north side of finger five; all of the activity was on the south side facing the bridge. I glanced over my shoulder and thought I saw some activity behind us but we were engaged in what was happening on the south side.

Soon tracers were coming from the hill firing at our rear flank.

The next day we would learn that while were engaging the enemy on the south side, a group of Viet Cong were sneaking up behind us from the north slope. They would have had an easy, clear shot at the light and the grunts and could have pinned down the tank. They would have taken us out in seconds.

A Marine was standing guard on the hill, watching our firefight and saw the silhouettes of the VC coming up behind us. He opened fire with the 30MM machine gun on a tank, took out a few of them and chased the others away.

We had dodged another bullet.

After that we made sure we had a few men guarding our rear.

WHAT??

One night there was an extended firefight. We could not seem to discourage the enemy as we usually did. These were NVA Regulars, not the local VC and they were unrelenting.

Perhaps they needed additional time to move their ordinance. Since they had invested so much time and energy bringing their rockets, mortars and other weapons down from North Vietnam, it was logical that they would put whatever energy was needed into having them where they wanted them, when they wanted them.

The tank moved from our right flank to the left and back to the right again. I was following their movements but, not knowing what they were seeing or doing, I simply maintained my position. We could not communicate by radio so we mostly used hand signals and yelling.

I heard Skully, the Tank Commander, yell something and stuck my head up above the jeep to try and hear what he was saying. When I did I found myself looking down the barrel of the tank.

Skully had yelled, "Fire in the hole!" which was the signal that he was about to fire a round in a way that could impact us. He was right.

The reflexes kicked in and I ducked just as an explosion went over my head. I never heard the tank fire; I simply flew backwards for a few feet and landed on my butt.

As I got up I could hear almost nothing. It was like being under water and hearing muffled voices that were difficult to understand. The tank engine was a low roar, the jeep engine something of a whine and the machine gun a series of thuds.

I went back to the jeep and turned off the light. I had no way of knowing where to shine it and I was concerned I would light up some friendlies. Besides, the tank blast had blown the canvas top off of the jeep and I was not sure if it had created other damage as well.

The party was over anyway.

It turned out that the tank was taking orders from two sources because units were being hit on our right and on our left. That's why they had been moving. At one point, there was a key, strategic opportunity to take out an enemy position on our left but there was not time to move the tank. The TC had made the decision to fire over the jeep and had yelled his warning.

The next morning I went to the medic on the hill. His examination revealed that the gunk in my ears had been compacted during the blast and all that was needed was to clean the ears. A corpsman was assigned the job of pumping hot peroxide down the ears over and over again. Finally one ear cleared and he showed me the lump of debris that he had removed. Dust, dirt and even bugs would find their way into any available body cavity.

Eventually the other ear was cleared as well.

In some places this would have merited a Purple Heart; here we did not even have access to my medical records or any way of communicating with the folks in base camp. Who would want to explain their Purple Heart to the folks back home by talking about dirty ears anyway?

This was an indication that we were doing some pretty nasty things to our young bodies. If the monthly Malaria tablets' ability to dislodge our compacted bowels didn't do us in, what was a little grime in our ears, noses and mouths?

Besides, it was almost Christmastime and I was planning to be home for Christmas. I wasn't sure how that could happen and each passing day made it a little more obvious that it would take some special finagling to get me there.

## THE MOTHER OF ALL FIREFIGHTS

Charlie threw everything at us at once one night. We were taking fire from several different angles. The light was out so I moved the jeep out of harm's way and continued giving coordinates on the radio.

The unusually long party was taking its toll. I looked over at the tank and the turret was rotating 180 degrees between firings. This could only mean one thing: they were running out of ammunition and had to retrieve the rounds in the most hard-to-reach places in the tank's belly.

Martin had stopped firing.

There were fewer grunts returning fire.

The enemy was on our right flank behind a ridge line close enough to hear us talk. I was communicating with the command bunker by keying the microphone and had called in a barrage of mortar fire with the intent of either taking out Charlie or encouraging him to leave.

Obviously, it worked and the party ended.

A couple of squads were sent out to recon the area and find what was left of the enemy. During the extended party a Huey gunship had seen our tracers and had come over to help. He was one of the people Skully was communicating with during the firefight. We had used the 105 battery during the firefight and the 80MM mortars at the end.

The squads returned and gave a sit rep.

The Marines used three criteria for enemy casualties: Confirmed, Probable and Possible. A body or significant body part, like a head, would be a Confirmed. A lesser body part, like an arm or leg, would be a Probable and a blood trail would be a Possible.

I would need their count for my sit rep back to base camp in the morning. The 105's and the 80's also noted the count as did the Huey. Of course the grunts reported the same count. As a result, the enemy casualty list was multiplied each time one of us sent in our situation reports.

When people question the number of enemy killed, this is how the number gets exaggerated. When all of the situation reports are compiled somewhere, the folks doing the compiling cannot know who was where so they use simple arithmetic.

According to the sit reps, we may have killed more enemy soldiers than there were.

The best part of these relentless parties was that it took our minds off of Christmas and what we would be missing back home. If I caught myself thinking or humming a Christmas carol, I would stop intentionally. That was the kind of distraction that could get a man killed.

A letter from my mother explained that the boxes from my R&R excursion had arrived and would be stored until I got home. Then she went into detail about how she would keep the living room decorated with an artificial tree until I got home and we could all celebrate Christmas together.

The reality of being on Hill 55 for Christmas was sinking in and I did not like it.

During the party Martin had stopped firing because the machine gun had failed. At one point during the firefight a round had gone into the super-hot chamber and swelled up when it was fired. The extractor that was supposed to grab the empty shell and eject it held on to the empty casing while the bolt went back. The result was a broken bolt.

On our next trip to the rear I took the pieces of the bolt to the supply sergeant to get a replacement. He and I were discussing how the bolt had broken when the Old Man walked in.

"What happened to this?" He knew it was broken; I wasn't sure he knew what it was.

"A round jammed in the chamber, Sir," I began, "and the extractor held onto it when the bolt came back and sheared."

"What were you shooting at?"

It did not occur to me to explain that I was not shooting, Martin was, nor did it cross my mind I might want to think before I spoke. "Gooks," was my incorrect answer.

First of all, the Old Man was still not convinced we had any enemies in our sector and he forbade the use of the term "Gooks". I took my deserved dressing down and the supply sergeant and I continued our conversation after the captain left.

By the time Christmas Eve rolled around, Charles, the NVA, had backed off and we would go through an entire night with no parties. In some ways this was scarier than being hit since we knew they were still in the area and could hit us any time. It was a silent night but by no means holy.

The daily briefings almost always included a warning about the enemy's use of holidays for attacks. We were told they thought of us as uncaring drunkards and assumed we would be in no position to fight on special days when we had been celebrating. It never worked out that way; the enemy rarely engaged us on holidays – another sign the guerillas were using the predictable unpredictably.

I chose not to participate in the Christmas Day feast with the tank crew. It turns out that it was a large gathering and included people we did not know. I was content to stay at the bunker, follow my C-Rat dinner with some of my mother's stuffed cookies and read.

Unknowingly, like so many others, I was compartmentalizing many thoughts and emotions. The psychological shell, the armor, we wrapped around ourselves thickened over time. At first it was not learning much about the people around us so their demise would not take a piece of us with them. It was reinforced by thinking of the Vietnamese as something less than human to make it easier to pull the trigger and to endure the results. The assumption was, I think, that we could simply remove the shell when we went back to the World and resume our previous lives.

It was naïve thinking, of course, but we were naïve boys becoming men in a surreal world.

### The Old Man Makes Nice

Our second trip to the rear that month was supposed to be something special. The USO Show would be held in the assembly area and we were allowed to schedule our routine maintenance on the day of the show.

We left Hill 55 as soon as the roads had been swept for mines and made our way to base camp. A couple of miles from our destination we hit the traffic. There was never traffic this time of morning but this day it was jammed. Trucks of all sizes, jeeps, Mighty Mites and men walking had the roads all but closed. Everyone wanted to see the USO Show.

By the time we reached base camp we agreed that the crowd was too much and there would be no seating anywhere near the place. Some people had camped out for a couple of days to have a good seat. We would just have the techs service the jeeps, make a resupply run to the PX and mess tent and go back to the hill.

We were greeted with bad news. The techs were at the show; we were expected to perform our own maintenance. And there was worse news: the Old Man wanted to see me. Corporal Clark was the bearer of this news flash.

Walking over to the orderly room I was trying to think of what I had done wrong this time. He was probably still ticked about the "Gook" remark, we looked less-than-military with our worn uniforms but that was nothing new. He still had the windshield with the bullet hole only now it was waxed and shiny.

"Sergeant Reaves reporting, Sir."

"Sit down, Sergeant."

He sounded pleasant. He began by asking how we were doing. I assumed he was on drugs. He had never shown interest in our welfare before. Then he pulled out a brown official Army file folder and began going through it. This is where he would have noted the times he wrote me up, the threats of court martial for my various offenses and who knows what else.

"You have distinguished yourself, Sergeant Reaves. You have the makings of a good career soldier."

Oh, no. This was a reenlistment talk.

He actually thought I would consider making a career of the Army after experiencing the year in Nam. Of course, he had a quota to meet and they had given me a promotion so he would have an E-5 on his list if I said yes.

I listened to the reasons why a military career would be a good thing for "someone like you". He had already calculated my re-enlistment bonus and it would almost cover the cost of the Buick that would be waiting for me at home. Of course, as a soldier I would not have many opportunities to drive it.

I told him I did not think the Army was right for me and he bore down.

He asked what I intended to do when I returned to the States. I told him I would be getting married and using the G.I. Bill to go back to college.

He saw his opening. "Oh, that won't work. You will have a young wife who wants to go out and you will have to stay home and study. That can be hard on a marriage."

Before I could stop my tongue I said, "At least I'd be there, not half way around the world."

The word was out that the Old Man's wife had filed for divorce. While he had been in Nam she had found someone else. I knew that but did not think about it before speaking.

"You're dismissed!"

I left and actually felt bad about it all.

Back at the maintenance tent I found the other members of Station Break 44 leaning up against the Jeeps with their arms folded. They were not about to perform maintenance on the jeeps while the techs enjoyed the show. We decided to raid the mess tent, drive over to the PX and then head back to the hill. The jeep maintenance would just have to wait. If it wasn't important to the folks in the rear, it wasn't important to us.

We had missed a night's sleep to go to the rear and learn we would not see the USO show. We would not have the jeeps serviced. And, for me, I would further damage my relationship with the Old Man.

New Year's Eve was coming up and again we were warned about enemy attacks on our holidays. This was 1967 and 1968 would prove to be a pivotal year. Of course we could not know that at the time. All of our now-close comrades – the tank crew and some of the grunts – would rotate home in the new year and we often spoke about what we would do first when we got back to the World. I joked that I would flush some ice cubes down the toilet to prove I was home since I had not seen ice cubes or a flushing toilet in so long.

1968 was an election year and President Johnson would announce that he would not run for reelection. His announcement stunned everyone. He would have been a shoo-in for the Democratic nomination and the polls showed that despite the unpopularity of the War, he was seen as the best person for the job.

The stress of what the Vietnam War was doing to the country was concentrated in the White House and no right-thinking person who knew what was really going on would have any interest in the position of President. Generally, politicians have not been numbered among the right-thinking people but we elect them anyway. After all, they spend more money earning the job than the job pays and, once in office, develop the same group-think mentality during the first half of their term and use the second half focusing on reelection.

President Johnson had taken over after the assassination of John Kennedy under whose leadership we began the slide into the hell of Vietnam even though Senator John Kennedy had said in the 1950's, *"How do you fight an enemy who is everywhere and nowhere?"* As a decorated and wounded World War II Navy PT Boat Captain, he understood conventional warfare and recognized the difference between conventional and guerilla warfare. Still, he allowed us to get involved.

The French had been in Vietnam, or Indo-China as it was known, and been defeated by the rag tag Viet Cong. We, as mighty Americans, assumed we could do better. We were proven wrong.

Forty years later we would make the same mistake by going into Afghanistan where the Russians had been defeated by a low-tech enemy. We, as mighty Americans, assumed we could do better.

## QUICK DRAW

One night during the week between Christmas and New Year's a hill due south of us was hit. It was a smaller outpost than Hill 55 and had a few grunts, a mortar battery and a sister tank to our tank crew. Being from the same unit, the men on our tank knew the other crew well and had trained with them in the States.

Every crew member on a tank is proud of their ability to perform their particular function and they can be very competitive. As the Tank Commander, Skully was proud of his tank, his crew and his record as he should have been. The driver, Dong, was proud of his ability to take the tank places where others would not and to never break the track.

Scab was the loader and a loader's claim to fame is how quickly they can ram a shell into the breach and have the tank ready to fire again.

The TC would have the driver put the tank into position, he would give the coordinates or target to the gunner who would aim the tube and then fire on the TC's command. As soon as a round fired, the breach on the back of the tube would come back into the tank, eject the spent shell and the loader would drop in another round and close the breach with a lever. The tank would be ready to fire again. Meanwhile, the loader would need to get rid of the spent shell, retrieve the next shell and be prepared to do it all over again. While the breach was open, gas from the tube would enter the tank so the loader wanted to quickly insert the next shell and close the breach.

Three seconds was considered good; anything less was outstanding.

We sat on the tank watching the party on the other hill. The tank fired and, under his breath, Scab counted, *"Thousand one, thousand two, thousand three"* and the tank fired again.

Skully took a drag on his cigarette and said, "He's pretty fast, Scab."

"I can do that." Scab was focused on the party – more interested in the performance of the other loader than anything else.

The distant tank fired again, and Scab nodded his head as he counted, "Thousand one, thousand two, thou..." and another round came out of the tank.

"He's pretty fast, Scab." Skully was having his fun.

By now we were all counting. The tank fired again and someone counted out loud, "Thousand..." and again we saw another blast from the tank.

We were dumbfounded; Scab was beside himself. He jumped off of the tank, threw his hat on the ground and began stomping it all the while screaming, "Nobody is that fast! Nobody is that fast!" We continued to laugh and harass him.

He was right, of course. It turned out that the other hill had been warned of an attack and a second tank had moved onto the hill. We were watching two tanks, not one. Skully had learned this earlier in the day but had not told anyone.

Scab settled down after that but his hat was never the same.

## **P.T.S.D.**

*Uncertainty can create mental trauma. The Viet Cong were becoming increasingly effective by using newer and crueler tactics. The North Vietnamese Army had moved into our area and was using more powerful and sophisticated weapons. By this time there was no room for emotions. If someone died, they died. Thinking about Christmas and other holidays brought a mixture of sadness and resentment. So we attempted to make the best of those special days by spending them with people who were disposable. The trauma of it all thickened our resolve not to care about anything.*

# CHAPTER FOURTEEN
## Short Timer

Hill 55, Month Ten, 30 Days to Go

S ome rules kicked in for me, rules I appreciated this time.

Anyone with less than a month remaining in Vietnam was considered to be a short timer. They were excused from going out on patrols and other dangerous duties. Those with one week remaining would go back to the rear and spend their last days in country sleeping nights and eating cooked food. It was an attempt to acclimate us to the World where we would be returning.

While I was still in charge of Station Break 44, Martin would take the leadership on finger five and I would stay on the hill, usually on the north side facing DaNang. There was little activity there and I spent my nights thinking about home, getting married – or not, the new Buick and mama's cooking.

This daydreaming could have dire consequences in a combat zone and the daydreaming is all but inevitable for the short timer - hence the need for rules for them.

Back in the summer a crisp, new second lieutenant had come out to the hill and ignored the short timer's rules. He not only ordered a grunt with less than a month left in country to go out on a patrol, he ordered him to walk point. The patrol returned to the hill later that day with one casualty, a fatality, the second lieutenant.

We were serious about not buying the farm late in the game.

My year in Nam was ending. I would stare out at the peaceful, green valley and see an occasional fighter jet burn its way into the clouds from the airbase.

Then one night there was a surreal scene. From the tree line on the other side of the valley, a rocket went airborne headed for DaNang. Flores was with me, saw the rocket and looked at me. I grabbed the mike and raised the command bunker. "Construe 24 this is Station Break 44, over."

Nothing.

I repeated, "Construe 24 this is Station Break 44, over."

A sleepy voice came back, "Ah, yeah, ah, 44, this is Construe 24, over."

"This is Break 44, observing rocket fire, stand by for coordinates, out."

An alert voice came back, "Roger, rocket fire, over. Ah, out." He was a bit addled but he was on the job now. Urgent radio messages have that impact; it's like having the phone ring in the middle of the night.

This would not be easy. I was using my well-worn map but I had not used a compass in so long I was having trouble remembering how to use it accurately. I could only generalize the location of the rocket launcher, especially since I was trying to remember where I had seen it go up and it was dark.

The NVA helped me out by launching several more rockets from the same location. My calculations were crude but I radioed them in anyway. There was some chatter on the radio as the 105's scrambled and put crews on all of the guns.

A few minutes later I heard a Mighty Mite coming down the hill to our position. A Marine captain came over and we talked about what we had observed and I showed him on the map where I thought the rockets might have been.

Enough of the rockets had gotten close enough to the airbase for them to scramble some jets. The captain was in communication with them and told me to point the light in the direction of the launchers. The jets made repeated passes over the area but saw no targets.

Some Huey gunships – new to the Marines at the time – followed but could not find targets either.

This had been an NVA training exercise. They were practicing for the all-out assault a few days later which would be their contribution to the beginning of the Tet Offensive. The Tet Offensive was the beginning of the end for America's participation in the war and for using Nam for man-building.

There was no way we could have known that.

All of us – the captain, the artillery, and the jet and helicopter pilots – were all pawns in a game our leaders were learning to play. The other side played the game better.

Looking back we can put together the pieces. The heavy activity during the previous weeks was designed as a distraction to move the rockets into the valley. The Tet Offensive would be a major, coordinated activity throughout South Vietnam when multiple major U.S. installations would be hit simultaneously. The guerilla war the enemy had been waging was morphing into a hybrid guerilla/conventional war and we were not prepared to address it.

Enemy activity picked up as my activity was also picking up. I was making my plans to go home and trying to make wedding plans with ushers and a best man. All of this had to be done by mail and now the mail deliveries were slowing down.

Two weeks before I was supposed to ship out I was ready to go to the rear. On my morning sit reps I would ask when my replacement was coming. Martin was running the unit and doing it well. I was ready to stand down.

Finally, a week before I was supposed to rotate home, I was supposed to already be in the rear sleeping nights and eating cooked food. It wasn't happening. In our nightly chats on an unused radio channel, Lindsey and I wondered why they were not relieving us. He was due to rotate at the same time I was.

Finally, with three days left in country, a truck came out, picked me up, dropped off Martin's newest responsibility and I began my trip home.

The platoon commander met me when I arrived in base camp. He had made First Lieutenant and was on his way to Captain. He escorted me over to the orderly room as we talked about going home and the year in Nam. We went into the Captain's office unannounced which surprised me until I realized the Old Man was not there.

"Captain Hayworth is on leave, uh, settling some personal matters," he began. "I'm acting CO so it is my privilege to tell you that tomorrow at 1300 hours there will be a formation, a Marine Colonel will be here to award you the Bronze Star."

He pulled some papers from another brown Army file folder. Holding a piece of paper he said, "This is the citation that will be read. Afterwards the Colonel will pin a ceremonial medal on your uniform. The real medal and associated documents will be sent to you back in the States."

I did not know how to react. So I didn't.

"You cannot wear that uniform. The supply sergeant has a new one for you. Congratulations."

Was he congratulating me for having a new uniform?

Lindsey showed up a few hours later and we went to chow together and stayed up most of the night. After all, our body clocks were set for sleeping in the mornings and staying up nights.

THE CEREMONY

There is a smell that accompanies new military uniforms. It had been a long time since the quartermaster at Fort Benning had introduced me to the aroma. As I pulled on the brand new socks, crisp new jungle pants and the fresh jungle fatigue shirt I was already feeling more human. I had showered with soap and hot water.

A brand new pair of jungle boots was on the floor next to the cot. For months we had begged for jungle boots and were some of the last to get them. It was aggravating to see the people delivering the mail with these cooler, steel-soled boots while we were still wearing the hot leather boots with a standard sole – one that punji stakes could easily penetrate.

Before pulling on the boots, I considered how I might be able to get them out to someone on Hill 55.

The entire battery was in formation, I was in my assigned position and when cued, I marched smartly – well, as smartly as someone who had not marched in a year – across the back of the group, made a smart "right face, marched forward, executed another right face, went a few more steps, halted and made a left face and stared the seasoned Marine colonel in the eye.

I popped a salute, he returned it and I dropped my hand to my side.

The citation was read by someone. I don't recall it all but there was a lot said about how I stood up during firefights, directed artillery fire while firing the M79 grenade launcher. In retrospect it sounds impressive. In all honesty, I thought it was what I was supposed to do.

The colonel pinned on the medal, said something, I saluted again, he returned it, and I did as smart a retreat as I could. It was over. A few minutes later we would hear a helicopter carrying the colonel back to wherever he had come from.

Killing time before supper, Lindsey and I talked and made sure we understood how we would make our way back to the United States. It would be a circuitous route from DaNang to Cam Rahn Bay and then to Fort Lewis, Washington where we would be discharged. It was tricky but, as usual, Lindsey had it all worked out.

From time to time some of the guys assigned to various jobs in base camp would stop and ask about war stories. I was surprised that Station Break 44 was something of a legend but I was not really interested in talking about it. I had too much on my mind.

I also had a stack of mail to read. Since mail delivery had been curtailed over the past couple of weeks, it had backed up.

After supper Lindsey and I retreated to the orderly room. Since the Old Man was not there and the other officers were at the officer's club, we could find some peace and quiet.

Sergeant Royal came in and joined in our conversation. He had arrived in Vietnam as an E-5 sergeant, the same rank that Lindsey and I had achieved, and he had been in the Army for six years. If he was resentful, I could not blame him.

At one point during the conversation he admitted that the reason we had not received our mail lately was that they were involved in a volleyball tournament.

It took a minute for that to soak in. At first I thought he was joking.

He wasn't.

I lost it. It is the only time I ever actually saw red. I remember screaming louder and louder. I turned over some file cabinets trying to get to him. I was going to kill him. All of the pent up rage from a year in Nam was now out in the open.

At first he smiled, thinking I was kidding around. When he realized how serious I was, he tried making his way to the door. I had seen the look that was now on his face, the look of a man staring at pending death.

Lindsey came up behind me, put me in a bear hug while I was screaming and while Sergeant Royal disappeared.

It is amazing how the body can change chemically during a rage like that. I never want to feel that again.

We began talking about our trip home the next day. That sort of cooled me down but I was still shivering as I nodded.

The End of the World

Lindsey and I sat and talked for several hours until what appeared to be the end of the world started. The Tet Offensive began that night. Our first indications were the multiple simultaneous explosions at the airbase. The enemy had coordinated throwing explosives on many of the fuel bladders at once. There were mushroom clouds as the JP4 fuel went up in colossal explosions.

Alarms went off. People began scrambling. The rear had not been hit during our time in Nam and this was one major party. And it was their first party.

Suddenly Lindsey and I were the resources of choice. We had more combat experience than anyone else in camp, most of whom had none.

There were people standing guard duty like they had learned in basic training. They had never fired a round while in Vietnam but they would have to now.

Our perimeter was our responsibility. The Marines would cover their areas of responsibility but we had to hold our own. We had one exposed flank and, unfortunately, it faced the air base. The enemy had made it clear they were at the air base in sufficient numbers and could easily come our way.

Someone had to go out to the point and Lindsey volunteered us.

"Are you crazy?" I asked. "We're going home tomorrow; why would we go out on point tonight? Let one of these rookies go!"

He looked me in the eye and said, "Look at these guys. Do you want to trust them to cover point tonight?"

There was some discussion about whether or not I could be trusted with a rifle but going out on point with no weapon was not an option.

The extensive party lasted all night. Massive explosions were accompanied by small arms fire. Some aircraft were able to launch and the back-and-forth was intensive.

When the sun came up, it was quiet and the people at the air base could assess the damage. It was disastrous. The casualties included the aircraft that were supposed to take us home.

PAPERWORK

For all intentions, Lindsey and I were out of the Army; we just needed to get home. For that we would need paperwork and lots of it.

After breakfast we walked over to the administrative area where a clerk would need to type up our paperwork. The smell of burned fuel, buildings and other things hung in the air. There was a lot of noise coming from the airbase as they used equipment to get the facility back up and running.

When we asked to speak to the clerk assigned to process our papers, we were told that he had pulled four hours of guard duty the night before and, as was standard practice in the rear, was relieved of duty for the day. We would have to return the next day.

Lindsey and I had pulled guard duty all night every night for a year and had sacrificed sleep on many occasions including the trips bringing the jeeps in for service. It was now time for Lindsey to lose it.

"Where does he sleep?" he yelled. I did not know what he had in mind but I knew I would back him up.

We found the PFC sound asleep in his bunk. We woke him and told him we needed our travel orders. He told us to come back the next day and he was not especially tactful in the way he worded his statement.

The sound of an M16 chambering a round is distinctive, something anyone who has trained with the rifle recognizes. The sound of two M16s chambering rounds at the same time will cause a PFC to jump out of his rack and cut travel orders. We never lowered our rifles and at one point he actually cried. We did not care. We were beyond caring.

Lindsey's orders had him leaving immediately; I would leave in the afternoon.

A quick trip to base camp to gather our duffle bags and we were off to DaNang air base. We hitch-hiked a ride on a Marine deuce-and-a-half – everyone was interested in helping everyone after what had happened the night before.

We were mostly interested in getting home. Perhaps we should have had more sympathy for those experiencing combat for the first time.

The air base was mostly mayhem. There was still some smoldering fires, bodies were lined up – some ours, some theirs. Most of the aircraft that had been on the ground the night before were too damaged to fly. The operational aircraft had flown in that morning. The runways were damaged but one was still serviceable.

The plane that was to take me to Cam Rahn Bay was a civilian charter. It was a mess and probably never flew again. I stopped every pilot I could find and asked which way they were going. Finally I found a Marine cargo pilot who was taking an empty C130 back to Cam Rahn Bay. He invited me along but he was going to go over to Pleiku to pick up a friend. That was fine; I would eventually get to place that would offer an exit from Nam.

The C-130 is designed to carry cargo so the belly is wide open making it one of the noisiest propeller-driven airplanes in the air. Along the sides of the fuselage is webbing where a person can sit. It is not designed for comfort and the noise on take-off is amazing.

As we descended into the runway at Pleiku, I heard a different noise and noticed light coming in from fresh holes in the fuselage. The pilot pulled up, made another pass and had the same results. He changed course and we headed directly for Cam Rahn Bay. After we landed he told me that his passenger in Pleiku "was a friend not but that good a friend."

Cam Rahn Bay had been hit the night before as well but had not sustained as much damage. It was more fortified than the air base at DaNang and had been able to repel the attacks more effectively. It was mostly Army rather than Marine so it did not take long to find someone who could help me find a way to Fort Lewis, Washington.

I joined about fifty others who were also mustering out. There was a plane coming in around midnight and that would be our ride home. I prayed that it would not meet the same fate as the one in DaNang.

We gave up our rifles, were debriefed by a colonel and instructed on what we could and could not say when we got home. Our duffle bags were searched and most of our things were taken from us. We would not be allowed to wear fatigues because of the fear we would contaminate the airplane so we changed into our wrinkled khaki dress uniforms.

We found a mess hall, ate and went as a group to wait for our ride. Sitting outside the hangar we could hear some gunfire off in the distance and it became clear who in our group had seen combat and who had not.

A Boeing 707 commercial chartered airplane landed without any lights on and taxied over to where we were sitting. It was beautiful. I almost cried.

After it was serviced, we climbed the steps and saw civilization. Onboard were several female flight attendants, stewardesses as they were called. They volunteered for this service. God bless them.

They smiled and served drinks with ice.

We flew to Tokyo and changed planes in the wee hours. From there we flew to Anchorage and landed at the civilian airport.

The plane had developed some kind of a mechanical problem.

We had to deplane but the airport authorities would not allow us in the terminal. We were known to bring home diseases like Malaria, so the airport's management was just being cautious. It was February and many of us were seeing more snow than we had ever seen before while standing outside in our short-sleeved shirts.

The repair would take some time so we were invited into an isolated room and told not to leave.

By crossing the International Date Line we had gained back a day but the delay in Anchorage took away much of it. Finally we were underway and landed in Seattle after dark. We taxied beyond the civilian terminal, parked near a hangar at the end of the airport and steps were rolled up to the door. We had been told to remain seated.

An officer came up the stairs and made a few announcements. If we were mustering out of the Army we were to board the bus on the left. If we still had time to serve, we were to board the bus on the right. In either case, we were to ignore all civilians and not engage them in any way.

That was a strange request, I thought.

We walked quickly to the waiting buses. It was cold and we were in short sleeves.

There were civilians; many, many civilians. They had signs, some were singing and most were shouting. They were extremely loud. An Army person was standing by the door of the bus on the left waving us in. That's when I noticed a squad of Army grunts standing guard.

Once on the bus I chose a window seat and got a good look at the people and the signs. Both were ugly. Now I understood what a war protestor was.

While the bus loaded, I looked out and saw an American college-aged girl for the first time in a year. I smiled, she spat, and as the bus drove away I got my first look at Seattle through her spittle on the window.

24 And Out

It probably looked good on paper.

When the military wants to be efficient, it can be. The "24 And Out" program was designed to muster out returning veterans in twenty-four hours. We would not be delayed on our journey home.

In retrospect, a time of debriefing and decompression would have been better. Most World War II combatants came home on troop ships which took weeks. That was a quality decompression experience and was probably more valuable than we realize.

From the bus we went straight to quartermaster and handed them the envelope of travel orders we had been given in Nam. With all of the precision of an assembly line, we were measured for a dress uniform, "winter greens". Then we were transported to a mess hall for a steak dinner. It wasn't much of a steak but it was an effort we appreciated.

Finally we were taken to a barracks for a long hot shower and a quiet night's sleep.

We were awakened gently the next morning and given plenty of time to shower and to put back on our khaki uniforms. Then we were bused to a mess hall for breakfast. There were no formations and few formalities. We were not saluting officers and they seemed to understand. After all, we had not saluted officers for the past year.

Next was a physical, a very thorough physical since the Army would be responsible for anything that went wrong with us while we were in their care. Then there was a psychological exam which lasted maybe fifteen minutes as we were processed in groups of five.

The rest of the morning was slow. We had lunch, stood in line to have our final orders cut and then went to the paymaster for travelling money. Next we went to the travel office and were given a one-way ticket back to where the Army had found us. Mine was an airplane ticket since we were in Seattle and home was Atlanta. Some were given bus tickets.

We were escorted back to the barracks to gather our belongings which now amounted to almost nothing. Nothing that is, except for the new dress uniform. Somehow the Army had managed to keep good enough manual records to have each of our uniforms militarily correct.

Mine was hanging on the end of a double bunk. Spit shined shoes were on the floor and I had not shined them.

A military uniform is like a book. It can be read by anyone who understands the language. The sergeant stripes were exactly where they were supposed to be, the artillery insignia, the ribbons on the left breast were exactly placed. Above my name tag on the right breast were two unit citations: one for supporting the Marines in DaNang and one for Operation Arizona. The unit crests on the epaulets had green bands below them and a smart red/green rope ran around the left shoulder. Two service bars on one sleeve and two combat bars on the other rounded out the uniform. Everything fit like a glove.

One final task and we would be civilians. We were taken to a room, raised our right hands and spoke whatever it was we were told to say.

We went to the transportation center where our copies of our final orders would be brought to us and we could take any of the scheduled shuttles to the airport, in my case, or the bus station.

After an hour had passed we began asking where our final orders were. Okay, we were not asking, we were belligerent. We had flights to make and buses to catch. We had been away from home for a year and being this close, every minute counted. Another hour passed and we had formed a mob. Someone made the mistake of telling us that a Staff Sergeant who had our orders in his vehicle may have stopped at the NCO Club. So we came unglued and asked where the NCO Club was.

A Brigadier General was called in to quell the near-riot and soon our orders arrived by an officer accompanied by armed soldiers.

With the envelope finally in my hand, I boarded the last olive drab bus I would ever have to ride for the trip to the Seattle-Tacoma Airport. The first flight would take me to Dallas and the second to Atlanta. My time in Nam would be over, I thought.

In fact, it was just beginning.

## P.T.S.D.

*Suppressing the trauma had begun. Receiving the medal was an acknowledgement that maybe what we were doing had some merit. The clean clothes and new boots made me more human especially after having had the first hot shower in months. Part of me wanted to tell the military what to do with their medal; another part decided to take it as I had taken everything else the military had dished out. The incident in the orderly room when I attempted to kill the platoon sergeant should have been a clear signal – a siren –*

*that something was wrong. However, there was no process at that time for detecting this, probably because there was no program for treating it. Arriving back in the states and seeing first-hand the protestors at the airport and being neglected by an uncaring NCO helped to solidify the value of suppressing the feelings. Following WW II, the warriors returned home on ships and had weeks to de-compress. Vietnam warriors were told how lucky they were to have a 24-and-out: being out of the Army in twenty-four hours. Nothing made sense, so we shut down mentally, emotionally, spiritually and, to some degree, physically. For the military we were out of sight and out of mind.*

# CHAPTER FIFTEEN

## Homeward Bound

Few people expected the Atlanta Airport to become the world's busiest.

As traffic increased, the airport expanded to keep up with the demand. When rotundas became popular, the airport added rotundas. When straight, aluminum gateways were popular, those were added. As a result there was a mishmash of gates connected by a confusing maze of walkways that led to an overworked terminal.

There were a few peculiar gates and I would arrive at one of those on the Friday of a week that had seen me on Hill 55 on Tuesday, being decorated and celebrating Tet on Wednesday, travelling to Seattle on the first Thursday of that week and, thanks to the International Date Line spending the second Thursday mustering out and now arriving back home Friday morning.

Nothing was making sense.

The layover in Dallas had lasted from after midnight until the first flight to Atlanta in the morning. I could not sleep and spent the time in a bar drinking Coca-Cola and talking to a pilot who had just survived a plane crash. Understandably, he wanted to talk about his situation, not mine.

I had a center seat on the flight to Atlanta. My dress uniform stood out and I was leery of how people would react after the experience in Seattle. At one point I pulled out the case containing the Bronze Star and found a copy of the citation that had been read at the ceremony folded neatly inside. As I read it I noticed the guy next to me reading it as well. He said nothing.

There was no airport security in those days so the whole family was at the gate waiting for me. Hugs and kisses all around were followed by the drive back to the parent's home in Grant Park. Things were moving too rapidly for me.

In a letter my mother had asked what I wanted to eat when I got home. I gave her a description of the perfect meal down to the banana pudding for dessert and she had it ready at lunchtime.

After lunch my father asked if I wanted to go pick up my car. The dealership had called a few days earlier to tell us it was in. He drove my fiancé and me to the dealership, we completed some paperwork and I was behind the wheel of a magnificent automobile headed back to my folk's house.

I hit the freeway at a breakneck thirty-five miles an hour.

For more than a year I had not been in a vehicle going more than forty miles an hour and then only when Martin was driving us back to the hill. Jeeps are not designed for speed.

Since the driveway would only accommodate one car, my dad parked his car on the street so I could nudge the new Buick into the safety of the driveway. I stared at the car for a few minutes, not really sure of what I was seeing, and went inside.

My mother was standing on the porch. She put her arm around me and said, "Not bad for a first car, is it? You deserve it."

We watched the evening news on the black and white television and, of course, most of it centered on Vietnam. There was speculation about the sudden increase in hostilities in Nam and the ongoing hostilities on the streets at home. Some of the footage was real; some was staged. I assumed everyone could tell the difference.

Early in the evening I was tired, strangely tired, and suggested I drive my fiancé home. Once in the car she held up a stack of wedding invitations and asked if we should mail them. I was not prepared to deal with that issue or much of anything else so I said yes, took her home and went back to my folk's house and to bed.

I was asleep early by almost anyone's standards.

When I awoke the sun was setting. I had slept a deep, deep sleep for nearly an entire day. There was conversation coming from the room where the television was airing a game show. I stood up, looked out the window and saw the Buick. Someone had laid out some of my clothes from the pre-Army days and I pulled them on and went to join the others.

The usual, "Well, it's about time!" and "Sleeping Beauty is up!" greeted me. I sat on the sofa next to my fiancé who had come over hours earlier thinking I would be up. Of course my mother asked immediately what I wanted to eat. Leftovers from the day before sounded great.

There was something of a fog around all of this. The nightly news once again focused on Nam and criticized President Johnson as they would until he announced he would not run for reelection.

I commented on the news reports about Nam but found little interest from anyone. My mother was just happy I was home and whatever had happened was done and that was that. My father, the veteran, had nothing to say and my fiancé only wanted to talk about the wedding.

A new program would be on that night, one they were sure I would enjoy. It was called "Laugh In" which took its name from the sit-ins that had been changing our culture. It was amusing. Some of the humor was lost on me – people had to explain why it was funny. I had missed many cultural subtleties. It was obvious my ability to laugh would take some coaching.

Over the next weeks I would assimilate back into civilian life. We found an apartment we would move into after the wedding and we bought some furnishings.

I went job hunting. Going back to school was not appealing. I would follow up on ads from the paper only to learn too many were sales jobs and I was not at all interested in sales.

Job interviews were sometimes done in groups and on one occasion I was being interviewed with two other guys who were about my age. This was to allow the interviewer to more easily find the pick of the litter by seeing us side-by-side.

I was the third to be questioned. When the interviewer asked what my previous job had been I said, simply, "Vietnam". It had taken too long to explain what I had been doing during other in-terviews so I just abbreviated it to "Vietnam".

At that moment, the other two applicants moved their chairs away from me.

I was not offered a job with that company. On my next interview I changed the one-word answer to "Mercenary" figuring it wouldn't make much difference.

Since the military had given me extensive training in electronics, I went to Southern Bell, as Bell South was known in those days, and learned they had no openings. However, the nice lady said she thought AT&T was hiring.

It was the best career advice I could have received. For fifteen years I worked for the largest corporation in the world.

The first ten years I would remain in the same entry-level position they hired me into: a technician. Every morning for ten years I would put on my blue jeans, pack my lunch in a brown paper sack and go down to 51 Ivy Street for eight or sixteen hours a day. My military training and experience moved me up half-way on a six-year pay scale the day I started so there had been at least some benefit from the Army.

Few conversations about Vietnam ever occurred; not many people were interested.

During my first month on the job I received a certified letter from the Army. "A Bronze Star Medal and associated documents" were to be presented at Fort McPherson near Atlanta. I called the phone number on the letter as instructed. They would have a formation on the parade grounds; I would be awarded the real medal with my family and friends looking on. This would mean I would need to put on my uniform again, so I declined. All of the materials were placed in a box and dropped off at my apartment.

One day my boss's boss called me in his office and said it was time for me to move up. I had just passed my ten-year anniversary with the company; ten years of doing the same thing that new hires would be doing their first day on the job.

I thought I would go to engineering since that was the most logical course for a technician. Instead, he was sending me to sales. The career I had been offered several times when I got home from Nam was now being offered by my current employer. Obviously others saw something in me I had missed. My first full year as an Account Executive I was named as their top salesperson out of a group of 1,100 salespeople.

I was promoted to a sales management position, National Account Manager, and my team members wanted to know how they could be the top salesperson – what was my secret?

The secret was I never gave up. Something the military had taught me was helping me succeed in civilian life.

After leaving AT&T I wrote a book on persistence entitled, "The Theory of 21" and became a motivational speaker. One of my clients asked me to teach his salespeople how to sell so I added sales training to the repertoire. Working with senior executives all over the world led to the creation of new leadership curriculum, especially, Chief Sales Officer material. The confidence to speak in public and to sit face-to-face with CEOs despite my lack of education and experience all primarily resulted from my military experience.

A couple of years in the military would be good for most young men. Combat, an unfortunate by-product of military service, would not be good. When asked, I tell people I would not take a million dollars for what I learned yet you could not pay me a million dollars to do it again. The truth is, of course, if I was needed I would be there.

## My Old Best Friend Ray

Six month after arriving home I attended the funeral service for Ray Powell. There were no dignitaries there, no press and no fanfare. It was just another casualty of the Vietnam War as far as the world was concerned.

For his bride, his mother and the rest of his family, it was the end of their world.

In the eighth grade we had moved to Forest Park, a suburb of Atlanta, where my father would pastor his first full-time church. My sister and I would start a new school. During breaks, the boys would go outside and play a game. One boy would jump on another's back and try to knock down the others. I was new and shy so I was surprised when during one of the games another boy jumped on my back. We immediately charged into the fray to see who could knock off the boy on the other's back.

That was how Ray and I met. It turned out he lived a block away and so we became fast friends. We built model cars together, played football and, like all best friends, were inseparable. He was the oldest of four children and all of his siblings looked up to him. He would do anything for his brother and sisters – and for anyone else, for that matter.

Four years later my father was sent to another church sixty miles away so Ray and I communicated by mail. We got together from time to time but we were too young to drive and too far apart so the visits were rare.

Once we double-dated together – it was a blind date for both of us. My date said something unkind about Ray so I never asked her out again.

As soon as I got home from Nam he called to tell me he was getting married just before shipping out to Nam. For some reason, we could not find a way to meet. I regret that now, of course. As a result, I met his bride at his funeral.

It was a closed-casket service, of course. There was the obligatory 8x10 photograph taken of Ray when he was in basic training. This was one of the reasons why the military willingly provides the opportunity for warriors to have a good picture. The Basic Training picture would hang on his mother's wall in the room where she, like most mothers, would pray for her son's safety. It would be taken to the chapel for the funeral and then returned again to her wall.

I looked at his face and a flood of memories came back.

Ray had written home that he was in the hospital and would be fine and that no one was to worry about him. The letter was written by someone to whom Ray was dictating. He had stepped on a mine. When his mother had told me about the letter, somehow I knew Ray was not coming home.

That experience took the wind out of my sails; the war was not over after all.

AGENT ORANGE

The infamous defoliating chemical, Agent Orange, which was used extensively in Vietnam, had the capability of killing all plants that it touched. It did an awesome of job of what it was created to do.

Veterans wonder if their exposure to Agent Orange might have affected them and that seems to be a fair question. Since I lived on Hill 55 for ten months, a hill that had been completely defoliated with the stuff, the question crossed my mind from time to time.

My third child, my daughter, was born with an uncommon birth defect, Hirschsprung Disease. At the ripe old age of three days old, she was transferred to Egleston Children's Hospital, one of the finest in the country, which was associated with Emory University Hospital. A doctor there was one of the top two in the country for treating this rare disorder – such a coincidence!

The operations and the complications that followed caused her to spend a lot of time in and out of the hospital. The good news is that she recovered and is a healthy mom today.

The Centers for Disease Control, CDC, is located in Atlanta within walking distance of Egleston, Emory and the huge Veterans Administration Hospital complex. The CDC initiated a study to determine the effects of Agent Orange and I was interviewed and tested several times. I was told that the findings would be made known but when I tried to follow up I was told the study had been cancelled.

Today the CDC has good information on their web site about Agent Orange, mostly as it relates to non-Hodgkin's Lymphoma. While they refer to "previous studies", some of the data is not there and I probably could not understand it anyway. Wading through the information it shows that Vietnam veterans exposed to the defoliate had twice the occurrences of some diseases. However, when the population of Marines in Vietnam was compared to the general population, there was no statistical difference in the oc-currence of diseases.

The Marines were chosen because they were the primary warriors in I Corps where more Agent Orange was used. Hill 55 was in I Corps. What was seemingly omitted from the study was the fact that only one man in ten saw combat and only a small percentage of them were continually exposed to the defoliate.

It's one of those answers we will never have.

## Not the Same

Any idea that I could return home to the life I had been living before I was drafted went away during the first few weeks I was back. Every attachment to "normalcy" I thought I had was gone. Normal had changed and so had I.

I was forced to embrace the culture in which I found myself but few were willing or able to understand the culture I was leaving. Some guys wanted to hear blood-and-guts stories but most people were satisfied with a "that was then, this is now" approach.

Things are different in today's military. Communication has greatly improved so that even on the other side of the planet the combatant can take time out and visit with their family through audio and video services. The time it takes to communicate is as short as the quality of the communication is high.

Still, families back in the States must learn to function without the missing warrior and the warrior must be able to accept the changes of the family dynamics when they return. It is a complicated process, one that deserves professional help.

Neither the combatant nor the folks back home should expect things to be the same. They can, however, expect things to be better than ever if they take a proactive approach.

PTSD

Post-Traumatic Stress Disorder is real.

It manifests itself in different ways and at different time intervals. It is not the same for any two people so there is no one-size-fits-all cure.

Previous generations of veterans were either unaware of the disorder or thought it to be a sign of weakness. Fortunately, we have learned a lot about diagnosing and are making strides in treatment..

On one end of the spectrum are returning veterans who never talk about their experience. On the other end are veterans who can talk about little else. Most people fall somewhere in between. There are healthy and unhealthy people all along the spectrum. The willingness or unwillingness to talk has little to do with the psychological health of the returning veteran.

The *inability* to talk about it is a different matter.

Most vets will be more open with other veterans. We think they understand. It is easy for combat vets to discern if the other veterans actually saw combat or not and that flavors the conversation.

There are many programs for veterans and most of them are volunteer and non-profit organizations. A few have allowed me to be involved and, as a result, I've been named "Veteran's Advocate of the Year", an "Outstanding Georgia Citizen" and have been invited to the White House twice. My contribution has been miniscule compared to others.

Through this work I have learned how to recognize some of the signs of PTSD in other people and in myself. It can creep up on a vet and strike at the oddest times and in the oddest ways. For me, looking through binoculars was a problem for many years. Fireworks were intolerable and some still give me trouble, especially red flares and erratic firecrackers.

Recently I came out of the mall at night and three helicopters flew over in formation. I don't know what happened; I just knew I was frozen, could not get to my car a few feet away and was, even after forty-five years, desperate for an M16. It passed, but it was uncomfortable and I was glad no one was looking. Difficulty with relationships and suicidal thoughts plagued me for years.

I am fortunate to be married to a woman who earned a master's degree with honors in Christian counseling. She was among those who did not understand the war and all she and her friends wanted to do was "give peace a chance". Like most, she now recognizes that neither of us was right and neither was wrong.

A healthy, balanced mental attitude is essential. I believe that a growing belief in God is also critical for continual healing.

PTSD is treatable and it must be treated. It will not go away by itself.

A qualified counselor can, literally, work wonders in the life of the wounded warrior, the "walking wounded". They cannot and will never understand the trauma inflicted by combat any more than they can understand the trauma their other clients have faced.

But they know how to help the victim address it.

A medical doctor does not have to have had a broken arm to know how to treat it. The combat veteran who resists treating their PTSD because they think the other person will not understand does not, themselves, understand the value of solid counseling. Professional counselors have not personally experienced the specific issues most of their clients have and they are still effective in bringing about genuine healing.

When professional counseling is combined with participation in specific support groups, recovery can be rapid and significant. Many groups exist and there will be some close to any veteran.

## SUMMARY

Some statisticians have reported that for every person killed by hostile action in Vietnam, ten came home and killed themselves. Previous wars may have had similar results. Left unaddressed or untreated, the scars of war can worsen. Acknowledging there is a wound and understanding its cause are the first two steps in healing.

There are similarities and differences in all wars. As our culture and technologies advance, the impact of combat changes. Still, in some ways, there is consistency in what sparks PTSD. Here are a few ideas to consider.

### Abandonment

For most warriors there is a sense of abandonment while they are in the service. They are away from their loved ones who once had daily – even hourly – contact with them. When those contacts are severed, as they must be, the warrior begins to lose those important connections.

The military promises to fill that void. "For the next eight weeks I will be your mama, your daddy, your girlfriend – the only person you need!" is the way the drill instructor introduces himself as the recruits get off the bus. Sure enough, before long he is in charge of everything and everything is provided: meals, clothes, schedules.

But what happens when the military stops providing and seemingly abandons the warrior?

In the Revolutionary War the military abandoned the troops and left them snowbound without boots. Their supreme commander, George Washington, said that if he had known how Congress would treat its soldiers he would never have taken the command.

The Revolutionary Soldier learned to scrounge for himself.

In the War Between the States, Yankees and Rebels received minimal support from the fledgling armies' supply channels. Family members would actually travel to the battlefield and deliver some of the basics like food and warm clothing.

When it was reported that Union soldiers had raided and looted homesteads and taken everything, it seemed barbaric. But after weeks or months of deprivation I can see how a sense of entitlement could have clouded their thinking. After all, they had been in the hell of war while others were "enjoying" the relative comfort of food and shelter.

In World War I the Doughboys were not properly equipped for trench warfare and many soldiers were lost due to preventable diseases like trench foot and pneumonia.

The Doughboys learned to scrounge for themselves.

In World War II the massive buildup of men and materials and the unbelievable resupply channels that were established still could not cope with the unprecedented scope of the war and its battles.

The World War II warriors found ways to make do.

In Korea there was little understanding of what a guerilla war could be. Using the latest technologies available at the time allowed the military to create Mobile Army Surgical Hospitals or MASH units. The concept put a higher level of medical treatment closer to the front lines. It was experimental and the units often lacked essentials. Not only did the doctors, nurses and medics learn how to work around their lack of needed equipment and materials, they pioneered new processes that saved many lives and limbs, processes that made their way into the mainstream medical facilities back in the States.

As they scrounged and made do, everyone benefitted, including the medical practitioners back home.

In the Vietnam War, abandonment was on the front page of the papers and was often the lead story on the nightly news. Being abandoned by the people we thought we were serving was as difficult as being abandoned by the people we thought were supposed to be serving us. Curtailed mail deliveries, lack of resupply, and even looks of disgust from others in our unit who had the benefit of regular showers took their toll.

We learned to improvise.

In the Iraq and Afghan Wars, warriors had to call on civilians back home for some of the armament they needed. The slow wheels in Washington crept along while warriors saw the results on the battlefields.

They asked for help and the country did what needed to be done to help them improvise.

## Guilt

For the combat veteran, guilt comes in different flavors.

What We Did

Guilt for what we did is the first. Looking back did we really have to blow away the old mama-san and papa-san's hooch? What about the ancient pagoda? And did the farmer really come out better after we killed his water buffalo?

The worst guilt for the combat veteran is being on the sending end of friendly fire. Knowing that you were responsible for taking out some of your own troops has to be the toughest guilt of all. Friendly fire results from a breakdown in communications and it is rarely the fault of the person actually pulling the trigger. Knowing that does little to alleviate the guilt.

What We Didn't Do

Was there one more thing we could have done to help a comrade? When the squad was pinned down and all we could see were tracers, could we have found out which were ours and which were the enemy's?

Survivor's Guilt

Why me? What about the guys who had wives and children back home? Why was I spared and they were not?

Many former war protestors have approached me and apologized because they feel guilty now about how they acted and reacted. That is a form of survivor's guilt and it is unwarranted. We were all doing what we thought was right at the time.

## *Shame*

We were proud to serve and we are proud of many of our accomplishments. However, we do carry shame for some of the things we did. In the heat of battle when survival is on the line, a warrior can do things that he or she might never have thought they were capable of doing.

Everyone does things they regret later and are ashamed of having done. The shame turns to disgrace when others learn of the behavior – when it is exposed to the world. So when the Vietnam veteran returned and heard, "baby killer!" shouted at them, a feeling of disgrace came over them. When the Mei Lei Massacre hit the headlines and people learned that hooches were burned and civilians were slaughtered, it hit a little too close to home for some veterans. Even though that was an extreme example of a cruel tactic used in Nam, others could relate to similar incidents during their service.

## *Purpose*

"Why?" is a very important question for the warrior going into battle and it is one they are not allowed to ask. "Ours not to reason why..." after all.

The establishment of America was a good reason to fight so the Revolutionary Army had purpose. Preserving the Union was a reason for both the Union and Confederate soldiers to fight. Saving Europe from a brutal regime was reason enough for the WWII soldier. In the Korean War, the purpose for fighting was not much clearer than the battle lines. In Vietnam we had been told about the domino effect of communism.

People will do the seemingly impossible when they understand why they are being asked to do it. We were indoctrinated (there is no other word for it) into the belief that communism had to be stopped and Vietnam was the front line. We heard a lot about the "war in Indo-China", the "Domino Effect" and other concepts that sounded noble and important but we barely understood them.

Jerry Coffee, a POW in the Hanoi Hilton and now a powerful motivational speaker, refers to the Wall, the Vietnam Memorial in Washington, D.C. by saying, "That wall had to go up so the Berlin Wall could come down."

Perhaps the Vietnam War was not all for nothing.

## *Rules*

War is war; there are no rules. Despite the best intentions of generations of lawmakers, rules are made to be broken on the battlefield.

The only rule in a knife fight is, "Bring a gun." Fighting some-one using their rules will not work.

British officers were stunned to find themselves the intentional targets of the colonists. Until then, the rules of war put officers off-limits.

Both Union and Rebel soldiers committed atrocities. In all subsequent wars, POW camps were not managed by the rules of war any more than interrogations in the field were. Torturing one enemy soldier in order to save scores of our own seems like the right trade-off. The list of broken rules is long.

The problem is that rules of war don't work and rule-breaking increases as the war increases.


JERRY COFFEE

Jerry Coffee was a POW in the Hanoi Hilton for seven years; more than five of them in solitary confinement. He was a Navy reconnaissance pilot. He and his second seat would fly over North Vietnam, take some pictures and return to their aircraft carrier where there was hot food and clean sheets.

One night their nightmare, every combat pilot's nightmare, came true.

Anyone who has heard his impactful motivational speech has been touched by his experience and, even more, by the person he has become.

We met in Washington, D.C. at the National Speakers Association Convention twenty years ago. We talked for a while and decided to go to "The Wall", the Vietnam Memorial. It is the only time either of us has been able to withstand the emotion of that experience. Even though we are in D.C and even on The Mall frequently, we stay away from The Wall.

That night we talked about our experiences as only two combat veterans can. At the end of our conversation, I said, "Jerry, I could not have done what you did."

He stared at me and replied, "I could not have done what you did."

We nodded at each other and then agreed on a significant point which is how we greet each other now. "You've gotta' do what you've gotta' do."

By the grace of God, we are both among the thousands who are still homeward bound.

## P.T.S.D.

*Sitting alone in the Seattle airport, the fog in my mind settled in. The next day I would have lunch at home with my family. There would be ice cubes and flushing toilets – things I had missed. The man sitting at the table in the chair where the boy once sat would have to acclimate quickly. Part of him wanted to resume where the boy had left off as if the previous year had been a bad dream – something that never really happened. Simultaneously proud and ashamed of his behavior over the past months, he did not know how to act, how to react and how to answer questions.*

*For me the P.T.S.D. had permeated my being mentally, physically and spiritually. My thinking would be forever flavored by the experiences in Nam. Sometimes this would be a good thing; other times it would be problematic. Physically I could not look through* binoculars, hold a firearm and had a low tolerance for fireworks. I had embraced the fine art of profanity while in Nam and would now need to cease the practice. Spiritually I had developed the ability to see people as subhuman. First it was the Viet Cong and the NVA – after all, it made it easier to pull the trigger or call in the artillery. Later it would be the local Vietnamese civilians. Finally, it would extend to those in authority and those in the rear who seemingly took so little interest in our survival.

Once home, how was I supposed to act and think? And, what was God's opinion of me?

# CHAPTER SIXTEEN
## Winners and Heroes

*There are no extraordinary people; there are only ordinary people who are doing things that others perceive to be extraordinary.*

In our culture we give medals to two entities: Winners and Heroes. Each earns their medals using the same basic process but their motivation, their driving force is different. Which would you choose to be? If you had the opportunity to be known as a winner or as a hero, which would appeal to you more? The world needs both.

A comparison of the two might help you decide.

The picture of Michael Phelps with a collection of Olympic gold medals around his neck and a big smile on his face is difficult to forget – or to misinterpret. He had spent a lifetime practicing, being coached, competing and then practicing and being coached some more. He focused on some of the finest points of competitive swimming since the difference in the gold medal and no medal can be a fraction of a second. He was a winner of the highest degree in Olympic swimming.

America loves winners. When the hometown team wins the Superbowl or the World Series or the Stanley Cup, many of the citizens earn bragging rights and they associate with the players on the team. The municipality holds a parade and ordinary people wear the team's colors and jerseys just so they can be a part of a winning team.

Winners receive medals for outperforming others in their field.

We also award medals to people who perform heroic acts. So what is the difference?

Both categories earn their medals using the same process which can best be understood using the letters in the word, "MEDAL".

### M – MENTAL ATTITUDE

By now you have probably been inundated with books, speakers and multimedia presentations about the importance of having a positive mental attitude. Every one of those messages is important because we are humans and are, therefore, subject to the frailties of human nature. Some of these frailties prevent us from becoming winners or heroes.

The number one attribute of human nature is habitual behavior. Habits are neither good nor bad, they are simply conditioned behavior. We do some things out of habit that are good for us – like the way we brush our teeth or the way we operate equipment. We can also develop negative habits and, from time to time, we all need the kick in the rear that causes us to stop doing those things that are holding us back and/or to begin doing the things that will take our success to the next level.

Thoughts always precede actions. Always. We will hear people say something like, "It happened so fast I didn't have time to think." Actually, they did have time to think – it just did not have time to rise to the conscious level. Our subconscious minds control much more of our lives than we may understand. That's why the positive mental attitude adjustment is needed from time to time.

There were times in Vietnam when I would realize we were in the middle of a firefight and I could not remember when it began. The first incoming round prompted a series of actions and reactions that had all of us performing our respective roles immediately – seemingly without thinking. This habitual behavior contributed to our being able to return home.

The three-pound organism in your cranial cavity is a remarkable device. Your brain can process information quickly, it runs all types of bodily functions without your being involved and it can trip you up if you are not careful. Every year new studies are published that reveal how remarkable the mind really is and, at the same time, acknowledging how little we know about its true functionality.

Earning a medal begins in the mind whether it is the result of winning or heroics.

Some of my friends who are avid golfers say that 90% of the game is played in the mind while others tell me that 80% is played in the tall grass. There is a lot of information for the professional golfer to remember on each shot. Their skeletal system must be in exactly the right pose while their muscular system operates exactly as prescribed. The grip on the club, their distance from the ball, the height of the tee and every gesture from the back swing to the follow through must be thought through. The pro knows what will happen if any of those actions are not right and they can correct them on the next shot, if necessary.

Heroes do not enjoy the opportunity to think through what they will do ahead of time as thoroughly as winners do. Nor are there do-overs or mulligans for the hero. Most often, the opportunity to be a hero is thrust upon them unexpectedly. Their actions may, in fact, be reactions. They will say later that they were just doing what seemed right, what anyone else would do in the same situation.

You see them interviewed on the news programs on television. The young man who jumped on the subway tracks to save someone who had fallen does not see it as a big deal. The mayor who ran into a burning house and carried someone to safety claims to have done what anyone else would have done.

So the mental attitude of a person who earns a medal, whether they are a winner or hero, is one of "successful outcome". They believe – not think, believe – that something good can come from the situation. The difference, then, is forethought. The winner sees himself or herself standing on the podium receiving the gold medal days, weeks, maybe even months before the race. The hero has only a short amount of time to evaluate the "contest" and to consider the best possible outcome. The hero rarely considers what reward will follow their actions.

### E – Excellence

When seeking excellence, everybody does not get a trophy.

It is trendy in some places to give everyone a prize. The thinking is that we don't want little Johnny to feel bad if others won a prize and he did not. Winners and heroes have little patience with that mode of thinking. The winner needs for someone to lose in order for them to win. After all, if everyone gets a trophy, why run or jump or swim at your best?

Bob Richards was a popular motivational speaker in the 1960's. He was fond of telling the story of Roger Bannister, the first person to break the four-minute mile. He would tell his audience that the way Bannister was able to achieve that seemingly impossible accomplishment was by running twelve miles a day, every day. Then he would challenge each person in the audience with this question, "Would you like to know how you can break Bannister's record? Thirteen miles a day!"

What brings us success today will not bring us success in the future. In fact, what brings us success today may actually cause us to fail in the future. It is not a matter of *being* something; it is the process of *becoming* something that earns respect, admiration and medals.

The definition of excellence in any category is fluid – it is a continually rising standard.

Bob Richards was the first track and field star to be featured on a box of Wheaties. He earned that "medal", if you will, by being the first person to pole vault fifteen feet. This was before the advent of the high-tech composite poles that are available today. After breaking the record, being awarded the medal and having the media attention a winner deserves, it all came apart. After the track meet, when the devices were being dismantled, it was discovered that the bar had been inadvertently set at fourteen feet, eleven inches. Richards had not broken the record after all. He had out-jumped every other athlete in the event but he had not broken the elusive fifteen-foot barrier.

How would you respond to that?

The next major track meet was held at Madison Square Garden and Richards vaulted fifteen feet <u>and one inch</u>. What had he been doing since the previous meet? He understood that excellence in pole vaulting would be an ever-increasing goal so he had been training for even higher levels of accomplishment. Such is the mindset of the winner.

Hero Goals

Heroes are not performing to do "just enough". That is not an acceptable standard for them. While in the throes of their heroics, their focus is on achieving the total win. The person who runs into the burning building does not try to carry the victim closer to the exit; their goal is to take them to unmistakable safety. While they may have little time to plan and strategize, the hero's goal is clear: win at all costs.

When we were under attack in Vietnam, our goal was never to lose as few people as possible; our goal was to cause the enemy to lose as many of their warriors as possible. In the sterile civilian world I live in now, that seems harsh, but combat heroes do not see it any other way.

## D – Diligence

The only difference in you and the person who is doing what you would like to do is just that: they are doing it. There are no extraordinary people; there are only ordinary people who are doing things that other people perceive to be extraordinary. Believe it or not, not giving up is considered to be extraordinary behavior.

Remember, there are plenty of people who want to **be** something; there are few people who are willing to **become** something.

There is a price to pay for being a winner and for becoming the hero. The winner enjoys the luxury of time in counting the cost and determining whether the payback will be worth it. The hero typically does not.

My wife is a fan of figure skating so I watch the competitions with her and try to understand and appreciate it all. What does sink in with me are the "fluff pieces", the back stories that are aired between the performances. They show how the skaters would be on their local ice rinks every day before school started and again after school. Weekends and holidays would find them skating and fine-tuning each minute detail. There was a price to pay for their medals, and they stuck it out until the price was paid in full.

A popular line from the heroic movie, "*Apollo Thirteen*", was "Failure is not an option". For the hero, if one approach does not work, they will try another. The outcome is clear; the outcome is success, not failure, however success is defined at that moment. They do what it takes. After all, you gotta' do what you gotta' do.

Jerry Coffee talks about successful missions he and his "second seat" ran only to find that weather obscured their ability to find their aircraft carrier in the Tonkin Gulf. If flying through the storm did not work they would try flying over it or under it. They would skim above the water's surface looking for a silhouette or search for the algae that was stirred up by the ship's propellers. They never gave up; failure was not an option.

Even on the night they were shot down, the two crewmen were discussing options, alternatives and ideas for keeping their damaged aircraft aloft long enough to evade the enemy even as their plane plummeted towards the water.

For the winner and for the hero, giving up is not an option.

## A – ABILITY

Medals are earned as a result of increased abilities. Not only do winners and heroes continually improve what they know how to do; they learn to develop new abilities – and then to improve on those as well.

One capability many winners have is their willingness to develop the skill to calm their minds in spite of what is going on around them.

A former judge who is now a well-known and respected commentator for a news network was to give on-air feedback about a trial. The camera cut to her before she had been given her cue and there she was, not realizing she was on camera, taking deep breaths, eyes closed and calming herself. She then gave a comprehensive, energetic, detailed summary of the court proceedings she had witnessed.

Frantic minds can become panicky when the person does not know how to control it. Conversely, developing the ability to control the physical and mental processes helps a person perform optimally.

People who are winners or heroes for the long term are typically multi-disciplined. Their lives do not center around one activity. Yes, they are focused and disciplined and they pay the necessary price for their success; but that is not the sum total of who they are. We are all composed of a physical, mental and physical self. That means you have the same composition as any winner or hero you know. What are you doing to develop each of these?

Lee Iacocca was a winner in business. He took a moribund Chrysler corporation from near collapse to being a strong and successful company. Under his leadership new classes of automobiles, including the minivan, were introduced. In his biography he mentioned his wife in a way that let the reader know that his home life was important, was a priority and was a counterbalance to his hard-charging, take-no-prisoners business approach.

The executive who refuses to develop his ability to use a computer will find himself or herself of little use to the business world despite their experience level. The salesperson who fails to update their communication skills will find their sales declining – and wondering why. We would not choose a surgeon or an attorney if we knew they were not continuously updating their knowledge and improving their abilities.

On Hill 55 our objective was to continuously improve our abilities to thwart whatever the enemy threw at us. That was an easy objective to set because the enemy also believed in Continuous Quality Improvement, CQI, as we now know it. They were devising more ways of taking us out of the "game" and we were devising more ways of taking them out. Sometimes we could win by practicing as Martin did with the machine gun. Other times it took heroics – spur of the moment actions as we reacted to new threats. The key was always, "better this time than last time".

Learn new ways of doing new things and you can join the ranks of winners and heroes.

## L – Legacy

"What do you want on your tombstone?"

The question threw me off my game. A technology company in Ohio had put several hundred of their people through a twelve-week video training program with me as the talking head.

Afterwards, they brought a few hundred into an auditorium for a question-and-answer session which I was to facilitate. Most of the questions centered on the training but when one woman stood up and asked hers, I probably looked like a deer in the headlights. "What do you want on your tombstone?"

I deflected the question by saying, "I want it to say, 'He was real old!'" While that elicited a laugh, it also began some contemplation about what legacy any of us are going to leave behind.

We know we "can't take it with us". So all of the material things we accumulate will probably be worth whatever the yard sale brings after we're gone. Any accumulated wealth will be distributed to others and then all that will remain is what we have instilled in the hearts and the minds of the people we have touched.

Who are the people you can touch on a regular basis? Who are the random folks who cross your path? We touch more people than we realize and, too often, we are careless about how we impact their lives.

The winner has more control over their legacy than the hero. After all, the winner can prepare – practice, train, study – for the moment when they will earn their medal. They can dream about receiving the recognition and about telling their grandkids how they won the race.

But the hero has their opportunity thrust upon them. The hero does not have time to prepare for how their actions will contribute to their legacy; they are totally in the moment. However, once the event is over and the adrenaline has subsided, the hero has a deep sense of accomplishment which, for most, is enough of a legacy.

M.E.D.A.L. – Mental attitude, Excellence, Diligence, Ability and Legacy are the hallmarks of winners and heroes.

### YOUR HEROES

A more fundamental difference between the winner and the hero emerges when we examine motivation. One is motivated by self, the other by others. Winners seek acclaim for themselves, the sense of having proved to themselves and others that they can be the best. This is important. Everyone should strive to be their best and the winner's medal is a visual acknowledgement of their achievement.

The hero earns their medal by serving others.

To better understand the mindset of the hero, use the letters H.E.R.O.: Help, Encourage and Respect Others.

### H – HELP

It is the desire to help another person that creates heroes. This is obvious when we consider the person who runs into a burning building to save someone. But how does it apply in the military? Is the solider, Marine or other serviceman really thinking about others when they do whatever it is they do to earn a medal?

This took some thought. After all, the night I earned my medal I was just doing what I thought I was supposed to be doing.

Or was I?

On more than one occasion I put Martin in for a medal. True, he enjoyed firing a machine gun more than anyone else ever could. Should he have been rewarded for enjoying his job?

What settled the issue in my mind was remembering the conversations we would have after the firefights. Once the hill had been quiet for a while, the casualties removed and the adrenaline was dropping, we would kill the jeep's engine and the tank would shut down theirs. The silence would be deafening.

Martin and I would make some coffee with the consistency of engine oil – and a taste to match – and wander over to the tank. "We survived another one," "We gotta' get out of this place," and "Nice job, Doggie" followed by, "Nice job Gyrene," were the themes of our conversations. Then we would talk about how to fight better next time.

We did not want to be close to any of the others but during these conversations it became clear that we were, in fact, each other's keepers. During the firefights I believed that each of them was doing all they could to protect everyone else and I intended to do the same. My role was to do whatever I was able to do to help the other warriors do whatever they were able to do.

In combat, it is not every man for himself; it is every man helping every other man.

## E – ENCOURAGE

Heroes have no interest in putting down or otherwise discouraging or disparaging others. There is nothing to be gained from making someone else look bad. In fact, we cannot hold a person down unless we're willing to stay down with them.

Even the men – well, boys really – that I fought beside in Vietnam who just could not muster the nerve to do what needed to be done did not deserve to be taunted. They needed to be encouraged because we needed their help. Some would respond to gentle encouragement like giving them a simple assignment during the firefight. "Go back to the bunker and bring us some ammo!" Others had to be physically encouraged – okay, forced – to do the right thing. Grabbing them by the collar and forcing them to do something they did not want to do was a form of encouragement.

Even Chumley, the guy from the rear who wound up sliding down the hill face first because he disobeyed orders was not treated as a coward or a loser. The following morning when the truck from the rear came out to pick him up I was too tired to be nice to him. So it may have seemed to him that I was not supportive or encouraging to him. Back in the rear he turned the experience into a positive, rethought his ideas and was eventually assigned to an outpost where he performed admirably.

Anyone can criticize. Heroes do not invest time in finding fault with others. Most are painfully aware of their own shortcomings and see no need in pointing out the flaws in others.

## R – Respect

Heroes maintain respect for the people they help and encourage. There is no consideration of "better-than-you" in the mind of the true hero. Their motivation is simple: at some time all of us need a hero. Therefore, helping others is the right thing to do.

In fact, not helping contributes to a lack of self-respect. The opportunity to be a hero is an opportunity to <u>improve</u> one's self-respect as well as their respect for others.

Have you ever had the opportunity to help someone, hesitated, and then while you were waiting someone else came along and did the good deed? How did that feel? Would you have respected yourself more if you had acted more quickly?

Some people simply cannot accept help. They find it demeaning to have to depend on someone else for virtually anything.

Maybe their pride or their self-esteem keeps them from accepting the aid that could benefit them. This can also be because the person helping them takes a better-than-you attitude.

Heroes know that at some time everyone needs help. It is a weak person who cannot accept help and it is a weaker person who shows any level of condescension to the person they are helping.

Heroes know it is a privilege to serve. We respect people who give us privileges.

## O – OTHERS

It's not about you. Rick Warren began his best-selling book, *"The Purpose Driven Life"*, with those four words. The world does not revolve around anybody; it revolves <u>because of everybody</u>. Everyone has a role to contribute and most people are trying their best to fulfill their responsibility. On the other hand, everyone needs a little help now and then.

I believe that it is a part of your purpose to be someone's hero.

The person who concentrates more on others than on themselves is the perfect candidate for heroism. Do not confuse putting others first as a sign of low self-esteem. And do not see it as martyrdom. Heroes do not think that way. Instead, the mindset of the hero is, "We all do what we can." Today I may have the ability to lift someone up and then tomorrow they will be in a position to help me.

That is the thinking – but not the reality. In fact, the people who are aided by the hero are rarely the ones who return to help the hero. But they often do become heroes for someone else.

So, who is your hero and whose hero are you?

## BE A HERO

It is not uncommon for us to think of our parents as heroes, or maybe our teacher, pastor or coach. Those are people who invested in us because there was some relationship and maybe some sort of responsibility involved.

Opportunities for heroics abound if we will just look for them. It will probably not be a burning building you run into but will more likely be a kind word, a few dollars given in the right situation or a seemingly simple gesture.

The opportunities are there – just don't expect a medal or even a thank you. Anonymous heroics are often the most impactful.

The car ahead of us was speeding, had cut us off and was zigzagging in and out of lanes when it hit the guardrail, went airborne and disappeared down an embankment. Most of the cars on the Interstate continued on their way. Several cars pulled over and some of us scampered down the hill through the wet grass and found that the car was empty. The driver was lying in a ditch a few yards away so we made our way there as fast as we could. I grabbed the handkerchief out of my pocket and used it to close a gap in his forehead. Another man jumped into the ditch to hold the drivers legs to stop him from thrashing and further hurting himself.

As often happens, the car's engine was still running even though the vehicle was on its side. "Can someone turn off the engine?" I yelled and then realized the other man and I were the only two nearby. The others were standing at the top of the hill. Finally, one person came down, turned off the car's engine, took a look at the three of us in the ditch and then made his way back up the hill.

The paramedics were great when they arrived. They quickly assessed what was going on, stabilized the victim and said they needed to get him to a hospital quickly. The other gentleman who had stopped to help, the paramedics and I struggled to carry the stretcher up the hill. We kept slipping and falling until a couple of burly men in dirty tee shirts and coveralls who had just arrived reached out their plate-sized, calloused hands and pulled all of us up at once.

While squatting in the ditch waiting for the paramedics, I learned that the other gentleman was a salesperson from out of town driving a rental car to a hotel nearby and had a big presentation the next day. He was wearing the suit and tie he had planned to wear for his big day and now the trousers were wet and grass stained.

It didn't matter. It did not matter that the driver was stoned and had been a danger to everyone on the road that day. It did not matter that no one would ever know that the salesman had helped unless he decided to tell them.

It only mattered that he was a hero.

The seemingly smallest gestures can make you a hero to someone – even if someone else receives the credit. After all, there is an old maxim that states, "It is amazing what you can accomplish if you don't care who gets the credit."

The Atlanta airport is confusing to many travelers. Those of us who are in and out of it frequently find an opportunity to help misguided travelers on virtually every trip.

Two unsophisticated, inner-city young women were staring at a sign and were near tears. The security line had taken longer than they thought, and now they were in danger of missing their flight. Meanwhile, they had no idea how to find their way to their gate.

"May I help you?" I say that a lot in the Atlanta airport.

They explained their situation, showed me their boarding passes and I escorted them to the correct train, rode with them to their concourse and explained how to find the right gate. As they exited, one turned to the other and said, "I told you Jesus would send someone to help."

On a busy section of the Interstate my car came up on some debris in the road. With cars on both sides, I had no option but to run over it causing a blowout on the left rear tire. I could nudge the car to the side of the road next the guardrail but there was not enough room to safely change the tire with cars streaming close by at high speed. I called for help and while waiting for it to arrive a street gang pulled up behind my car. I locked the doors and cracked the driver's window a few inches. One man said they would change the tire for me. Dressed immaculately for a gang, and not appearing to have strong mechanical skills, I decided the only thing they were likely to change was the ownership of my wallet.

Was I misjudging them?

When I lifted my phone and explained that I had called the police to block the lane as well as roadside assistance, they quickly retreated to their car and sped away.

Interestingly, the truck that arrived to change the tire was a "H.E.R.O." vehicle. These are the unique and celebrated fleet of Highway Emergency Response Operators who patrol the Atlanta roads offering assistance to anyone at any time and at no charge. Real heroes, wouldn't you say?

SUMMARY

The world needs more winners and heroes.

Don't be shy. Don't let past failures or embarrassments hold you back. Look for opportunities to serve others. The bystanders who stood by as the stranger and I attended to the driver of the wrecked vehicle were not sure what to do so they did nothing. If that is how you might have reacted, consider taking some first aid courses. If you typically rush through the airport ignoring those people who are seemingly disoriented, becoming a hero to someone may be easier than you think. If you would like to make a career or an avocation out of being a hero, there are plenty of volunteer organizations that will welcome you with open arms.

After all, there are no extraordinary people; there are only ordinary people who are doing things that other people perceive to be extraordinary.

# CHAPTER SEVENTEEN
## Next Assignment

If you are one of the people with PTSD or if you know someone who is, there is a step that must be made. PTSD does not cure itself. Help is needed and help is available.

There are many organizations that have as their core purpose helping returning veterans. There are independent counselors who can help people work through their specific PTSD issues. Some churches and civic groups also offer resources to help.

In other words, there is no excuse for not seeking help.

Many Vietnam veterans, like their World War II counterparts, are of the era when seeking mental help was a sign of weakness. Real men don't go crying to a counselor, they think.

Just the opposite is true. Real men will stand up and face their enemy even when the enemy is PTSD.

Whatever resource you choose, check them out to see if you think they can best understand and address your specific PTSD. In my business activities I have seen how much money some of these organizations spend on fund raising. Spending a million dollars on a television ad or a mailing to solicit ten-dollar monthly contributions does not seem to make a lot of sense sometimes.

Personally, I work for and support those organizations that rely on significant volunteer help. Not only does this hold down their administrative costs, it also shows that other people believe in their work enough to donate their time as well as their other resources.

Seek help if you need it, provide help if you know how and/or support those who are providing the help our heroes deserve.

Chuck Reaves, CSP, CPAE
Chuck@ChuckReaves.com
770.965.5595 M: 404.822.6171
www.ManInNam.com

Made in the USA
Lexington, KY
05 March 2017